Love,
Lisa

LISA K. LOCKE

Love, Lisa

VISION PRESS

Library of Congress Cataloging-in-Publication Data
Locke, Lisa K. (Lisa Knight), 1964-
   Love, Lisa / Lisa K. Locke.
         p. cm.
   ISBN 0-9628579-0-4 : $10.95
   1. Locke, William Mattison, 1964-1987. 2. Locke, Lisa K. (Lisa Knight), 1964- . 3. Christian biography—United States.
   4. Cancer—Patients—United States—Biography. I. Title.
BR1725.L62L63 1991
248.8'6'092—dc20
[B]   91-22699
                                   CIP

1 2 3 4 5 9 VP 5 4 3 2 1
Printed in the United States of America

Vision Press, Inc.
P.O. Box 1889, Cheyenne, Wyoming 82003

Acknowledgments

"You turned my wailing into dancing;
You removed my sackcloth and clothed me with joy,
that my heart may sing to You and not be silent.
O Lord my God, I will give You thanks forever"
(Psalm 30:11-12).

And so I do. I thank God my Father and the Lord Jesus Christ for the story, the words, the orchestration of circumstances. How He has blessed me with many good things!

There are so many individuals, families, and churches who gave of their time, finances, and especially themselves during Matt's illness and following his death. The love of the Father was flowing through you. There could never be enough thank yous.

Where would I be without my family's support? Thank you, Dad, Mom, Sandy, Joe, and Becky (and sister-in-law Lorie and niece Jessica, too) for your patience and understanding and for giving me the space and freedom to be who I am.

My "other family," Larry and Judy, along with the whole Locke and Ramey families—you will always hold a very special place in my heart. Thank you for sharing Matt with me.

Melanie Meadow spent hours reviewing the manuscript, offering suggestions, making corrections, listening to my heart. Mel, I will never forget the day at the church with you and me, my guitar, the computer, and the holy presence of God. Thank you, immensely so.

Two inspired gifts I received straight from the heart of God. Thank you, Jim and Lynne, for the guitar. The music has stirred things deep inside and drawn out the creativity of the Father. Don and Susan, thank you for the computer—a gift that keeps on giving. You have richly blessed me in your generosity and thoughtfulness.

The staff of the National Cancer Institute went beyond the call of duty to serve both Matt and me. Thank you for the loving care you provided throughout our time there.

The Clemson University family showed great concern for us, as well. Thank you for the special ways you demonstrated that concern.

Finally, to Sheri, my publisher, editor, friend: thank you for believing in me and in this story. I know the Lord is going to bless your ministry in the publishing business. You're the greatest! May we always marvel at the work of God.

P.S. Matt, still my heart is full of thanks for you. Thank you for giving yourself so completely to me. I am a wealthy woman to have been your wife, and my life is rich with memories of our time together. Until He comes....

FOREWORD

---

*"Precious in the sight of the Lord
is the death of His saints" (Psalm 116:15).*

Matt Locke was a young man destined for great things. Born and raised in Honea Path, South Carolina, he was blessed with a genuine love for his fellow man and a spiritual maturity far beyond his years. A born leader, he was elected president of the student body for both Belton-Honea Path High School and later Clemson University. I have no doubt that had he not been struck down at such a young age, he would have gone on to serve as a great leader of men.

I had the privilege of getting to know Matt personally while he worked as a page in my Washington office. I have never known a more conscientious or dedicated worker. He quickly won the respect and admiration of everyone with whom he came in contact, and his tragic death was indeed a great loss for us all.

I believe that Matt Locke will be remembered as a hero. His battle with cancer was hard fought. Throughout the ordeal, Matt continued to serve God and others by remaining the youth director for Pope Drive Baptist Church in Anderson, South Carolina. His courage held strong and his spirit was unwavering. In life and in death, Matt Locke served as a model for us all. I will be forever grateful that I had the opportunity to have known and been associated with such an exceptional human being.

I would like to commend Matt's wife, Lisa, for having the courage to share this heart-rending story with the world. I hope that *Love, Lisa* will inspire all who read it to follow the shining example which Matt Locke set for us through both his life and his death.

May God bless you all.

Strom Thurmond
United States Senate, South Carolina

Matt Locke with George Bush at Clemson University

September 16, 1985

There is so much I would like to go back and capture on paper, but there just doesn't seem to be time. Time—it scares me sometimes when I think about it, for it is constantly fleeting from me. Just as I reach out and take it in my grasp, it's gone to be seen no more.

So, here I now stand with but a moment that is actually mine. That's right, just a moment, for that is all we can hold within our limited grasp. All else is lost to the past or held in mystery by the future.

What am I going to do with the moments that are mine? Usually they are spent in idleness and that is not what I want. I desire for each moment to be spent wisely.

Father, grant me wisdom to know how important is time, and let me make the best of every moment You give me so that when they are all placed together, it can be said I had a life well spent.

—MATT LOCKE

The day dawned bright and beautiful—just like the hopes and dreams for our life together. Though the day was hot, it did not bother me to be wearing the long-sleeved white gown garnished with lace.

Standing with me, handsome as ever, was the one who had become the man of my dreams. His green eyes twinkled as he smiled at me.

Decorated with flowers and candles, the large church with padded burgundy pews was not full of people, but it was filled with something far greater—the presence of God. It was our wedding day, and the blue skies and sunshine reflected the joy of our spirits.   As we faced each other and vowed to love each

other for the rest of our lives, the joyful commitment showed in our smiles and tear-brightened eyes.

"Only God could love you more," sang our friend David with my sister Sandy as we lit the unity candle. As we were pronounced husband and wife that day, August 9, 1986, we knew fully that it was not this ceremony which made us one, but God Himself.

For months we had planned this day, talking, hoping, waiting. And with every bit of the exuberance of an Olympic athlete receiving his first gold medal, we relished the moments. Following the reception, we even felt like athletes as we raced to the car, facing a crowd laughing mischievously at the prospect of bombarding us with birdseed.

Our future looked as bright as the sky outside. We were in love with Jesus and in love with each other. We could hardly wait to discover the wonderful plans God held for our lives.

The car was covered with chocolate chip cookies, toilet paper, and toothpaste, but it offered shelter from the flying birdseed which the guests tossed joyfully at us. As we drove away from the church, Matt and I laughed and sighed. What a delightful morning it had been! As we left for our honeymoon, the skies began to grow cloudy. The rest of the day was overcast, but nothing could dampen our spirits. And so our wedding day came to a close, as beautiful as it began—in spite of the gray clouds and sprinkling rain.

Matt Locke was the most unique and exciting person I had ever known. Could I think that life with him would be anything less than unique and exciting, too? He had a zest for life that literally glowed through his personality and radiated in his smile. Unselfish and kind, strong, yet gentle, Matt's every action was characterized by his love for living, his love for people, and, above all other loves, his love for the Lord. Every day I spent with him was a new adventure in learning to squeeze the most out of every moment, in learning how to truly love.

We met as sophomores at Clemson University, and a close friendship soon blossomed into romance. Through most of our courtship our schedules were flooded with classes and jobs, studies and meetings. Matt was elected student body president for our senior year, and our time together became even more limited. When we did have a few minutes just to sit quietly together, we liked to dream about the adventurous excursions we would take someday. We even came up with a "one of these days" list on which we kept ideas for outings we wanted to make when we had the time.

We also spent a lot of time dreaming of our future together, but that didn't stop us from living to the hilt in the present. If anyone knew how to enjoy life to its fullest, it was this sandy-haired country boy from Honea Path, South Carolina. He could usually be found in the middle of campus events, from water-balloon fights to Christian gatherings, from political meetings to campus-sponsored activities. We busied ourselves with so many good things: university organizations, mission trips, classes, friends. That left us little opportunity to be alone together, so our honeymoon was a wonderful and long-awaited vacation for us both.

Twenty-four hours a day, it was just the two of us, even though the beaches of Cancún were fairly crowded. There were no schedules, no meetings, no one to interrupt our complete enjoyment of each other's company. We laughed a lot, and our never-ending smiles gave away our newlywed status. We basked in the sunshine, shopped for Mexican souvenirs, sampled the local cuisine, and true to Matt's style, made the most of every minute together. We knew our week in Mexico would pass by too quickly, so we felt obligated to create a honeymoon to remember. It was a glorious dream come true.

We returned to Matt's hometown and settled into a comfortable country lifestyle. We delighted in discovering the treasures of married life, and these were made even more precious because of our greatest treasure—knowing Jesus Christ as our Lord and Savior. He had brought us together, and we were determined that He would always be the foundation of our union. "Unless the Lord builds the house, its builders labor in vain" (Psalm 127:1). Trusting in the Lord to be the Head of our household, we knew our "labor" would not be in vain.

As husband and wife, Matt and I wanted to continue to grow together in every way. We read God's Word, knowing it held the instruction and counsel we needed for a godly life. We prayed together and saw how our spiritual intimacy was the deepest part of the life we shared. Our relationship with the Lord was reflected in the way we loved and responded to each other. "Now as the church submits to Christ, so also wives should submit to their husbands in everything. Husbands, love your wives, just as Christ loved the church and gave Himself up for her. For this reason a man will leave his father and mother and be united to his wife, and the two will become one flesh" (Ephesians 5:24-25, 31).

One time as Matt and I were kneeling in prayer, I could sense an urgency, a brokenness in him. Humbled, Matt was praying earnestly, "Whatever it takes, Lord, whatever it takes for me, for us, to be useful to You...."

Matt often seemed to be troubled about not knowing which direction God was leading us. Some time earlier, while we were in college, Matt had surrendered his life to the ministry. We knew that we were called to be ministers in whatever we did, wherever we went. We wanted to be open vessels for the Lord to pour Himself through to whoever needed us. But what were the specifics? What was the direction of our daily existence?

Matt had kept a journal for many years, and at one point after surrendering to the ministry, he was really feeling the pressures of school, student government, and his struggles with questions about life.

November 25, 1985

Matt Locke, just where is he now? I do not mean is he at home, or studying (boy, that would be news!), or out with friends. What I do mean is, just where is my life going right now?

I'm really at a crossroad point in the Life Path, and it seems that I'm at a standstill; I do not know where to go. I feel I'm running in place. I can't seem to get any traction; I'm just spinning my wheels. I seem to have no real purpose, no real goal to shoot for. Why? Have I left my first love?

Father, You were always there, ready to embrace me and to hold me tight with Your love. Now I can't seem to get back to You. I keep jumping in the way of my own progress. There are so many memories of shortcomings. So many failures I wish I could forget. What happened to my foundation? I know it didn't move, for it was like a rock; it was Jesus Christ. Now it seems I've taken a running leap off that foundation and landed in quicksand that is slowly dragging me down. Oh, Lord, please reach down Your hand and lift me out of this mire and muck in which I have placed myself....

Through the struggling, Matt was growing. Though he sometimes felt sinking sand beneath his feet as he took unsure steps forward, he was always taking small steps of faith in an ever closer walk with the Lord. Yet his humanness caused him to wrestle relentlessly with the question of his life's purpose. Thoughts of his reason for being continually preoccupied his mind.

March 14, 1986

Here I am in Alabama at Lisa's house.... It seems like it's going to be another busy spring break. I really need some time to relax, though. I just need to get away from it all.

I am having a rough time lately trying to decide what I'm supposed to do with my life after college.

Sounds like a good title for a book, <u>Is There Life after College?</u>

Lord, I need a lot of help to get out of my spiritual slump. Please, bring me out of this. I want to be back with You again.

The Lord often teaches us best when, after we have struggled, we realize the need for quiet stillness. A few days after that journal entry, Matt found a moment of quietness to notice the beauty of spring. Days later he would again write of his struggles with those same old questions, but for the moment there was peace and tranquility.

March 17

Boy, what a beautiful day! The birds are singing, the sun is shining brightly, making my eyes almost close in semi-slumber. It is so peaceful out here, and it places me in a state of great anticipation for the beauty and new life of spring that is yet to come.

I feel I'm in a springtime of my life right now. I'm just beginning to thaw from the cold winter that has preceded. My life is beginning to bloom again after it was seemingly dead for so long. It had been covered over with the cool crust of self-fulfillment, pride, and lack of determination to see life from God's perspective and not my own. I have such a long way to go to defrost my life and throw away all of the rottenness and fill it up again with good, healthy food.

Lord, bring me into the spring of life. Let me experience Your joy once again. Let me learn how to love as You do and teach me how to possess that trait of Yours, which we never seem able to possess, of how to "forgive and forget and continue to love." Make me more like You!

March 27

Here I stand before You, Lord, an imposter believing I'm something that I am not. I continuously try to fool myself into believing I'm something that I am not. I am not a super Christian, for I am not communicating with the One whom Christianity is all about. I seem to be afraid of something, and I can't figure out what it is. There are so many people expecting big things from me. All that really matters, though, is what You expect of me. What exactly do You expect from me, Father? I keep wanting specifics from You, but do I really have a right to expect that right now when I am not taking care of the generalities?

I need to be taking care of the generalities like trusting in You, studying Your Word, praying, and communicating what You mean to me to other people. Lord, show me how! I don't seem to know any more. I'm beginning to get so depressed. I feel so lost. Where to now?

A few months later, after graduating from Clemson, I was back in Alabama making final preparations for our wedding, and Matt was at home in South Carolina. The summer apart proved to be a time of growth and discovery for both of us. Matt captured his struggles in his journal whenever he had a few minutes alone.

May 11

I've graduated from college, so I've reached another milestone in my life. Even now, only two days after graduation, my heart is saddened, for I miss my friends, and especially Lisa. It feels weird being home again. In fact, it's driving me crazy. Here I've been in college for four years, able to come and go as I please and no one to tell me what to do. Now I feel like I'm facing culture shock again.

I also feel an uneasiness in my soul. The reason for this is my lack of knowledge of purpose. I cannot seem to pinpoint what I'm to do with my life. Am I really unconsciously running from something?

Tonight as I sat in church, I felt such a tugging at my heart, such a burden for those who are lost, such a desire to discover and live out all Christ meant for His followers to be.

I'm also a little scared about getting married. I'm very excited about it, too. I don't doubt Lisa is the one for me. I do not even doubt the timing. There's just so much I still feel I need to know. I feel so ignorant. Lord, help me, please.

Lord, open my blinded eyes that I may see the direction in which I should go.

May 12

"Breaking the Will": This is a point I have not come to in my life yet. I have not been broken. I continue to be too strong-willed, trying to do things my own way. I want to be broken if that's what it takes for the Lord to really be able to use me. I want the Lord to take my will and use me.

I feel the Lord is really dealing with me. I'm learning much this weekend about myself. I'm finding out how much I do not know and how far I still need to go in my walk with the Lord. Lord, bring me along. I want to know You intimately. I hunger and thirst to know all I can about living a life dedicated to You. Show me how to be holy!

May 14

There is a lot that I want to be different in my life, and I want it to go beyond my desires. I have such a long way to go in my spiritual maturity, and I have been doing absolutely nothing to increase my growth lately. I know if I want to grow I have to make it a moment by moment thing. I need to turn my daily routine over to my Father.

I talked to my "sweetie" tonight on the phone. It was great hearing her voice, and I would love to see her, but at the same time I'm pleased that we are away from each other. I want to be a different person when I see her again. Lord, make me different.

May 18

I just got off the phone with Lisa a while ago. I miss her something terrible. It's like having a part of me missing, and I know my happiness will not be complete until we are back together. Lord, just let me be for her what I should. Teach me how to love her.

I also have an uneasiness within my heart as far as a job goes. I don't know where to go from here. I feel the Lord pulling strongly upon my heart as far as the ministry goes. I feel that is the direction I am meant to go; it is just the timing I am concerned about. Lord, guide my paths. Let my decisions be the right ones. Help me Lord!

Love, Matt

Matt's mother recognized this uneasiness and talked with him about it. She advised him that it might be wise to wait on marriage, to find a secure job and work for a little while. But although he was unsure about his direction in life, he was sure about our marriage, including the timing. He told his mother he did not want to wait: "Something may happen, and I might never get to marry her, and I want to be with her." And in the meantime, God was continuing to work in Matt's life.

June 16

Defeat—it's a tough thing to face. It's something I haven't faced in a while. I've been given so much all of my life. In fact, I continue to be given a lot. There is so much that I have to be thankful for. I have a wonderful family, some great friends, a girlfriend who loves me, and most of all, a Lord who knows me and what I'm capable of.

It's really strange and stupid how I've left out the One that I say means the most to me. I've been making all of my decisions on my own. That is why I'm getting nowhere. I'm really worried now. Our wedding is 54 days from today, and I haven't found a permanent job yet. I fear tomorrow, but it's all because I haven't let God have today. I prayed for God to break me, but I never dreamed what it would be like. It hurts like crazy. I've been brought to my knees and have nowhere left to turn but to the Lord. I know now I cannot make it on my own. I also know life is much more than nine-to-five every day and riding a boat on the lake on the weekends. Our purpose is not to gain material wealth, but to increase our wealth of understanding in God. We were made to praise Him, to love Him, to serve Him. It brings Him, as well as us, happiness and joy for us to choose to serve Him in our own will.

Lord, show me what to do.

Preoccupied with wedding plans, visiting friends, involved in church, I neglected my own journal. But one entry reads:

May 27

Lord, I love You. And I want to focus on my relationship with You. God, I know the wedding plans have grown out of proportion, but I still want You at the center. You are the reason for our union to begin with, and I want more than anything for You to be the center of our home. I am trusting You, Lord, to make the necessary changes in me and in Matt...things are falling into place, but there's still so much to do.

Lord, I trust You with all of it! Matt's job, the wedding, this summer, all of it. Thank You for loving me unconditionally.

Love, Lisa

Matt and I also wrote to each other often, so I looked forward to the postman's arrival each day. And I stole as much time as I could to pour out my thoughts to him.

June 17

Dear Matt,
You are my favorite person in the whole world! To love you and to make you happy brings so much joy and satisfaction to my life, especially because I know this makes God happy, too!

I love you! And you know what else I love? Hugs, cuddling, staring into your beautiful green eyes, long walks, talking things out, back rubs, crying together, laughing together, experiencing LIFE with you! With Jesus as our Lord and Guide—won't it be challenging and exciting, sometimes painful, yet joyful?

I can't wait until we can live it, instead of just writing about it!

We were thankful to be able to trust our Lord Jesus to bring everything together. Matt and I both had productive summers, and we had an exhilarated and joyful spirit about our marriage. The wedding was beautiful, the honeymoon was glorious, and we were looking forward to a long and happy life together as man and wife. It seemed almost too good....

Our Sovereign God was and is in control, continually working for our good—for the good of His kingdom. His ways, His thoughts are higher and greater than ours. His wisdom is beyond compare. His love is fathomless. Doesn't such love, such wisdom, merit our trust in Him? This God, the one and only true God, would teach us deeper truths than we'd ever dreamed. "Call to me and I will answer you and tell you great and unsearchable things you do not know" (Jeremiah 33:3).

What was ahead? We did not know. But we knew God held us in His hands, for we belonged to Him. Even as the brightness and beauty of our wedding day faded into clouds, even as the laughter and smiles of our honeymoon turned to sadness and tears, He would teach us to keep trusting in Him.

A dear friend once told us that marriage is a crucible. God uses each partner as "sandpaper" to refine the other. Our union was a mirror of our relationship to Him, and daily we were put to the test of responding to each other in the love and manner of Christ. The same dear friend commented to Matt's mother, "He found someone who can go through the deep waters with him—and they're going to go through some deep waters."

Yet whatever "deep waters" were up ahead, we saw that circumstances and situations should not determine our attitudes; rather, we should purpose to obey every command of Christ. We were learning that we could choose to be joyful. We were learning that time is precious. We were learning how to live in the light of Jesus' love.

"Show me, O Lord, my life's end and the number of my days; let me know how fleeting is my life. You have made my days a mere handbreadth; the span of my years is as nothing before you. Each man's life is but a breath. Man is a mere phantom as he goes to and fro..." (Psalm 39:4-6).

An entry from my journal reveals the frustration we all sense in a fleeting life.

August 25

The days are passing so swiftly, Lord. Each moment seems to slip by as I dart from place to place, activity to activity, trying to find You in everything I do. My first two weeks—our first two weeks—of marriage have been great. We have so much fun together, and we can really share ourselves.

We shared ourselves in so many ways. We shared laughter and romance. Creative "meal dates"—which included Italian night in the dining room, sub sandwiches out on the porch swing, Chinese night in the living room at the coffee table (appropriately dressed in our bathrobes), and breakfast in bed, among others—lying out in the open fields under a starlit sky, or sitting outside on a Sunday afternoon sketching the scenery. We loved just being together.

Matt had a knack for making anything fun. I remember one night not long after we were married; he was busily pecking away at the typewriter in the study. The sporadic taps were intermingled with his silly, infectious giggle. He wouldn't allow me to see what he was doing until he produced the finished product, a small slip of paper with an exciting message—complete with typos and a play on my maiden name:

"William Mattison Locke and his wonderful wife Lisa were busing themselves around their cosy little 10 dollar a month house, preparing for an exciting xxxxx Knight (I crack myself up). In just a few moments they will loose themselves xxxxxx in a sea of passion for each other. Their Love will set sail to never dock again."

Matt and I tried to find pleasure in the little things in life. As with most newlyweds, we did not have an abundance of material things and great wealth. But that didn't matter to us. The Lord provided all we needed, as He would continue to do.

We had a beautiful home about three miles from where Matt grew up. Matt and his family had cleaned and repaired this house, which had been vacant for two years. It was a three-bedroom country home with a big front porch and railroad tracks fifty yards from the front door. We were renting for ten dollars a month from a dear ninety-one-year-old woman who also owned the surrounding property, her "home place." She herself lived in a nursing home. Being able to set up housekeeping in such a beautiful place was a dream come true for a couple of newlyweds rich in love but poor in cash!

The summer before our wedding and for a few weeks after the honeymoon, Matt had a desk job in an office that did not seem to suit this healthy, active man with seemingly unlimited energy. Matt's father owned and managed a home heating oil business, and sensing his son's frustration over a job, he offered Matt a position with his business. Matt readily accepted, and although his work did not exactly coincide with the political science degree he had earned in college, he did have the opportunity to work more closely with the public and to be outdoors.

Matt was a real "people person." He had an overflowing love for the people he noticed all around him. Never too busy to stop and chat, to carry a heavy load with someone, to laugh or cry with a friend—that was Matt Locke. He seemed to know everyone around town, and everyone loved and respected him. Everywhere I went, I was greeted with such comments as, "You sure got you a good one," or "We think the world of Matt. He's one of the finest young men around."

I received their compliments with appreciation. I was proud of my husband and that people knew what he stood for— what we stood for. Yet I was still trying to find my place in this new life. I wasn't unhappy or unfulfilled, but I was looking for whatever ministry the Lord might open up for me, in addition to being Matt's wife.

August 28

Lord, I'm searching for Your face,
Trying to find my place
            In Your will.

My Lord, as I seek You now,
Please come show me how
            To be still;

For I must learn the way of living crucified,
To die as Jesus died
            For me.

And I must live for You each day,
To open up and pray
            To Thee.

Lord, I am a child,
        Make me like Jesus.

Through the fleeting days there were so many moments to treasure, and I was thankful for all of them.

August 31

Lord, thank You for the moments in life....
The moments when I ask Matt to put the peanuts
up, and he puts them on top of the refrigerator.
The moments when I bring some old leftovers to
my mother-in-law's to feed to the dogs, and she warms
them up for the kids.

Moments when we thank You for the corn because that's all we had time to fix before the stove stopped working.

Moments when we take a romantic hot bath together, and the stopper handle connection breaks so the water won't drain out.

Lord, there have been so many wonderful moments. Teach me to cherish and savor each one...with You and with Matt and with everyone I come in contact with.

Thank You, God, for my wonderful husband! I am so in love with him. Nourish our love with Yours, God, and teach us to die so that Christ might live through us and in us.

Teach me, Lord, to be the most loving and encouraging wife. Help me to love Matt like You want me to and like I want to. He is a precious gift—second only to Christ. And I want to thank You, God, for each of the special moments with You and with him!

Love, Lisa

Matt entered his own thoughts into his journal that day, too.

Here I am, Lord, trying to keep my commitment of setting some time aside each day for just You and me. I didn't realize how much I need that daily time with You until this past year.

Forgive me, Lord, for not spending the time with You that I should. I miss talking to You like I used to, and I'm not about to go without that anymore.

Thanks for these past few weeks, also. They have been three of the greatest weeks of my life. I can't understand why some people don't enjoy marriage; maybe it's because they don't have You as a third partner. There is still a lot I have to learn when it comes to being married, but I sure am looking forward to learning.

Today we interviewed for the youth minister position at Pope Drive Baptist Church in Anderson and it went real good. Lord, if You mean for us to be there, just let the rest of it go great.

I'm a little scared about the possibility of getting the position. I know a little how Moses felt now. He was afraid because he didn't know what to say and was not good with words, but You provided him with all he needed, and I know You will give Lisa and me all we need, too.

Thanks, Lord, for a wonderful wife. Just let me be all that I need to be for her.

Matt and I were a very affectionate couple. We enjoyed expressing our love for each other in word, in deed, and in cards and letters. The little notes and phone calls throughout the day still brought those fluttering feelings in my heart, and Matt's gift with words could make me melt. He left me beautiful sentiments, and I recall one card in particular.

Dearest Love,

I think about you all day while I am at work, and I can't wait until I am at home with you. You bring a special joy to my life. Ever since August 9th my life has been much happier and more exciting. I look so forward to the many years we will share together as husband and wife. I could never be all I want to be for you, but all I am is yours and all we'll become will be a large part because of you. What will we become? A couple admired for their strong love for God, each other, and for others.

With Great Love and Admiration, Matt

His twenty-second birthday was September 3, 1986, and I had my love, my prayers, and a cross-stitched "I love you" to give to him. That morning I wrote in my journal:

Lord, each day is brighter and fuller when I start with You! I got off to an early start this morning—I got up at 5:40 and fixed Matt breakfast in bed. I really enjoyed doing that for him. I've been having a good time coming up with creative ways of showing my love for him.

Lord, show me how to let You work through all that I am and do for our marriage. I trust our future to You; show me "my place." I love You. Let this be a wonderful day for You and for Matt.

It is always refreshing to look back and see God's faithfulness to His Word and to our prayers. Five years earlier, Matt had written in his journal: *"Thanks, Father, for 16 wonderful years. Please let me use the rest of the years that I've got here on earth to serve You."*

The Lord honored both Matt's prayer of long ago and my prayer that morning.

That night we had his family over for dinner. We ate heartily, laughed heartily, and enjoyed celebrating. If he felt any pain or discomfort that night, Matt didn't mention it. He did say something about experiencing a shortness of breath, but we didn't really think much of it. It was, however, a small sign of something bigger. Soon the pain—physical and emotional—would become so great that he would finally have to take action. But for now, we all just enjoyed the birthday party.

God was preparing us for something, and He continued to chip away at what would not be pleasing or beneficial to Him. Matt felt it, too, and his journal reveals how the Lord was dealing with him:

September 8

Dear Heavenly Father,

I feel I'm being so slack in my commitment to You. Where are the fruits of my labor? They seem to be almost non-existent, and the only one I can blame is myself. I often think of all I should be doing. I should be praying more, I should be into the Word more, I should be meeting people's needs more.

Lord, show me how to make my future with Lisa brighter than our past. We have so many lofty thoughts of all that we are going to do for You, but lofty thoughts only float away if they are not carried out. Lord, just show us where to go.

Lord, forgive me, forgive me for my stupid pride. Here I sit staring at a plaque that reminds me of my "hey day," and I allow myself to become saddened some. I have no right to be proud of doing those things in the past. Without You, Father, all of them would have been impossible. Father, I place the future in Your hands. Take it, Lord, please.

September 24

Father, I praise You for the way You have been dealing with me lately. You sure are allowing me to get a good look at myself, and I'm not too pleased with the things I see. I see in me a long distance between myself and You, Father. My life looks nothing like the life of Jesus Christ. It just looks like the life of Matt Locke.

I want to accomplish something worthwhile, Lord. I want to do things for You with no desire for any self-gain. Lord, show me how to walk as Jesus walked. What am I to do with my life, Father? Return an excitement and purpose to me.

September 25

Being lax, the great art which the "Christians" of today have become well-seasoned at. We stand by and watch the world slap our religion in the face. Oftentimes we are given enough incentive to utter a slight remark about how bad things have gotten, but that is the end to our retaliation. I guess we all figure that the Lord can work it all out for Himself. We forget that we are the ones the Lord uses to wage warfare. He may fare better using the rocks and a donkey, for they don't worry about what others think of them. They don't have a community to impress or a friend they fear losing.

God was showing both Matt and me the necessity of a firm commitment to Him—there was no room for laxness.

The Lord had blessed Matt with a beautiful voice and a love for singing, and one of Matt's favorite songs was "We Are an Offering." He wanted more than anything for his life to be an offering of sweet fragrance to the Lord. How do we channel such desires into the actual serving and worshiping? Matt knew that his desires were right, but he saw that he needed to act on those desires. Pursuing God, yielding to the Almighty, Matt was aware that apart from Him we can do nothing (John 15:5).

"But thanks be to God, who always leads us in triumphal procession in Christ and through us spreads everywhere the fragrance of the knowledge of Him. For we are to God the aroma of Christ among those who are being saved and those who are perishing. To the one we are the smell of death; to the other, the fragrance of life. And who is equal to such a task? Unlike so many, we do not peddle the word of God for profit. On the contrary, in Christ we speak before God with sincerity, like men sent from God" (2 Corinthians 2:14-17).

A burning desire to be sincere, to be a real Christian, pervaded Matt's will. And he wanted to be the "fragrance of life" to those around him. The Lord had given us both a burden for teenagers, so when Matt was called to be the youth minister at Pope Drive Baptist Church in Anderson, South Carolina, we were challenged by the prospect of loving those young people and being to them an example of choosing life.

We immediately fell in love with the people there and knew God had made a special place for us in this church. The loving and friendly spirit at Pope Drive was evidence of the Lord's work. We looked forward to being a vital part of the Lord's ministry there. At the time we did not know the impact our lives would in turn have on the church.

The Thursday prior to our first Sunday at Pope Drive, an unexpected tragedy caused many in the Belton-Honea Path community to stop and take a look at their lives. A twenty-year-old girl died suddenly of a brain tumor. Headaches and nausea in the morning were the symptoms of a tumor that led to her death later that afternoon. Her fiancé was devastated. They were to finish school soon and had planned to get married in a matter of months. They had even begun furnishing their future home. In one short afternoon, their plans were drastically changed. As a believer in Jesus Christ, she was in her new home, her eternal home. The young man would have to go on to find his comfort, peace, and strength in the Lord.

Matt and I went to the funeral home to see the family. As they grieved with the young man, tears flowing freely, pouring their hearts out, we were saddened by their sorrow and the vivid reminder that life is brief.

When we returned home, we talked about the possibility of losing each other. "What would you do if I were to die?" we asked each other. Being newly married, we had a difficult time accepting the thought of remarriage for the other. But knowing that if one of us died, life must continue as God planned for the one still on earth, and because we were experiencing such joy in marriage with each other, we put away the selfish thoughts of the other not remarrying if God chose to take one of us home before the other. "But why think about these things now?" we reasoned. "Let us enjoy what God has given us in each other while we are together."

That weekend we made a trip to Clemson, visiting with some close friends and attending a football game. As we sat on the bleachers high in the stadium, Matt asked me to rub his back. It was really bothering him. Was it caused by the sofa bed we had slept on at our friends' apartment? He wasn't eating very well, either. But nothing seemed to slow him down. The four of us, Matt and I and our friends, went to a Bill Gaither Trio concert that night, and it was a joyful time of fellowship and worship. One song stood out to me as we listened to the beautiful music. "We have this moment to hold in our hands and to touch as it slips through our fingers like sand.

Yesterday's gone and tomorrow may never come, but we have this moment today." *And thank You, God, for today.*

The next day was our first Sunday at Pope Drive, and we were thankful for the opportunity to serve together. The church seemed to be excited about our coming. It was truly a ministering church, and in the months to come, we would realize this even more.

After taking the position at the church, Matt continued to work for his dad. With his full day of work and going to the church in the evenings, our time together became more precious and limited. We did make the opportunity to take a road trip to Clemson for the Fellowship of Christian Athletes meeting on Thursday, October 9. The new president of the university, Dr. Max Lennon, was speaking.

As president of the student body the previous year, Matt was able to help in the selection process for the university president. Through his work on the selection committee, Matt came to know the Lennons, and we both grew to love and appreciate them. We found out they were Christians, and we saw their lives reflect their commitment to the Lord.

That night Dr. Lennon spoke on setting priorities—the need to keep Jesus first. Mrs. Lennon was unable to come to the meeting; a close friend, who had recently become a widow, was visiting from Texas. So Matt and I, at Dr. Lennon's suggestion, stopped by their house to visit after the meeting.

As Dr. Lennon and Matt talked of my husband's call into the ministry and the possibilities of seminary, I spoke with Ruth Lennon and her friend about the frustrations I had with Matt's busy schedule. I remember the three of us sharing mutual feelings of the preciousness of time, the need to cherish the moments together, the commitment to treasure what was there.

Who would know this better than a woman whose husband had just died? Or the wife of a university professor with a rigid and busy schedule? I knew I could learn a lot from those two godly women.

We stayed rather late talking, but I left there feeling so thankful for what Matt and I had in each other and so hopeful for a bright future together.

With each day that passed, I became more and more aware of my love for this man who had so completely captivated my heart. In the few weeks we had been married, I learned to appreciate the way he shared himself with me. I loved to watch him, to listen to him as he interacted with other people, to hear him sing. His voice was strong, clear, and beautiful—much like him.

Though he had sung in many area churches and at several meetings of Christian organizations on campus, Matt and I had never sung together. We thought our second Sunday at Pope Drive would be a good opportunity. Matt was asked to do the special music, and he chose a song for both of us to sing. It was a song that reflected our commitment, a song we wanted to exemplify in our marriage.

"We'll build a household of faith that together we can make, and when the strong winds blow, it won't fall down. As one in Him we'll grow, and the whole world will know that we are a household of faith."

We looked at each other as we sang, and apparently our love was mirrored in our expressions. We heard several comments after the service. "That was beautiful, but were we supposed to be in there?" "It seemed like you two were all by yourselves." And we were singing to each other. We wanted to build a household of faith. But we didn't know the strong winds would begin to blow so soon...or so severely.

In the weeks after Matt's birthday party, when he first noticed a shortness of breath, he began to develop a nagging pain in his abdomen. He would not eat much, and I was sure it was my "new bride" cooking that was causing the problem. Then the discomfort increased, spreading through to his back. Nagging, gripping pain set in and robbed him of his sleep and his appetite. We spent several miserable nights trying to find comfort for him. Persistently, the pain refused to go away. Back rubs, muscle relaxers, hot baths—nothing relieved the constant ache. What was this thing that plagued him, that plagued us?

One of Matt's cousins was married to a doctor, and we consulted him often over that two-week period. Could it be muscle tension from the pressures of a new marriage, supporting a wife, paying the bills, the responsibility? Pills didn't seem to alleviate the pain. Could it be an ulcer? No, Matt tried the ulcer medicine and it didn't work. We decided to take the doctor's advice and have some tests run....

On Tuesday, October 14, Matt had several scans and x-rays taken. I had gone to my part-time job at a local department store before the results came back, quite confident that nothing was seriously wrong. I soon found out it was my nonchalant attitude that was seriously wrong. In the receiving room of the department store, I got a phone call from the doctor's office across the street. It was Fredda, Matt's cousin, who was a nurse there.

"Lisa, you need to get over here right away." I could hear the tension in her voice, its urgency startling me.

"Now?" I felt the lump rising in my throat. I started to feel hot, and I noticed that my hands were shaking. Hurriedly telling my boss that I needed to leave to check on my husband's test results, I rushed out the door and ran across the street. Fredda met me inside and led me down the small corridor toward Dr. Smith's office.

"This way," she directed.

Matt's mother, Judy, rounded the corner with her sister Nancy not far behind. The tense expression and the painful look in her eyes told me she already knew something, and that the news was not pleasant.

Silently we entered the tiny room. It seemed so dark. Maybe it was just the mood, or perhaps my anxiety about what the doctor would tell us. Judy knelt down beside me as I sat down. She patted my hand. What was going on?

Dr. Smith was calm and straightforward.

"The tests show that several of Matt's internal organs are enlarged," he explained.

He went on to discuss probable causes, such as a diseased gall bladder. He said the scans showed a sort of cloudy appearance, resembling a mass.

"There is a possibility that Matt has lymphoma."

"What does that mean?"

"It's a form of cancer." He continued to explain the type of cancer and some other information, but I could no longer hear him.

Cancer....

My vision blurred as the tears filled my eyes.

Cancer....

My body began to shake as a sob escaped my throat.

Cancer....

The very word pierced my heart. Such an ugly word. It made me think of darkness, of pain, of suffering...of death.

Judy was firm and determined. "We're gonna fight this thing." She hugged me tightly. Suddenly I noticed that she had been crying, too. Her son, her firstborn, could be suffering from a rare and deadly disease.

Matt was a very special son to Judy. Around the time that he committed his life to the ministry, his mother wrote him a long and heartfelt letter.

I've always known since you were a small boy that God had His hands on you—the long prayers when you even thanked God for the doorknob and toilets—to the way you'd go outside and talk to Him as if He were your favorite playmate, and all the questions of wisdom and understanding you asked. God has blessed you with a love for people and a need to serve Him. He has opened so many doors of service and growth for you. I promised God long ago that I'd be ready to let go when the time was right—but it seems that I'm not ready to let go yet. May God forgive me for my many human weaknesses. I'm afraid I love you too much—but that's a selfish love, and doesn't do credit to God or to you.

I'm glad He's directed you to a beautiful and fine Christian girl whom you want to spend your life with. Never let anyone or anything lead you away from your first love—God. God first, your wife and future children next, and others after that.

You're right—money and a supposedly secure life won't bring peace, joy, and contentment. There is no real security except in God.

Someone was talking to me the other day about all the tragedies of life. They said they didn't believe God could do all things or be all powerful or He wouldn't let people suffer and hurt or children die. I said I didn't understand why God let things happen—but I had the faith to believe that He has a reason and purpose for all things. I might not understand His purpose in this lifetime, but He would reveal it someday—maybe in heaven. I know I can tell when God's people are praying for me and when they don't—there are some who have a direct line open to heaven. God has a puzzle for my life and yours. All the pieces just aren't in place yet.

You have to forgive me for all my weaknesses—I'm too human. I often forget God and that's when I fall. The hardest battles of life are when we're fighting over our weaknesses.

You've always been a joy and pride to me. Your decisions have been sound, and I know they're based on God's direction for your life. Continue to keep your hand in His and always know, whether you're a minute away or a thousand hours away, my love and my prayers will always be with you—that will never end as long as I exist. Even when I'm gone from this world to God's world someday, my love for you will always remain. One thing you'll always know—God will never leave you or desert you. Even when you think no one's there and everything is dark and desperate, God is there. He knows. He cares. He loves. He lives! I love you!

A thousand thoughts must have raced through her mind, as they did mine, in the doctor's office that day. She must have thought about that little baby she held securely in her arms, the little boy climbing the tree or showing off his prize cow, the teenager standing firm for what he believed in even though few stood with him, the young man pursuing his dreams—dreams that might now never be realized.

"Does Matt know?"

"No, we wanted to tell you two first. We're calling someone to send Matt and Larry down here." Matt and his dad were together working on a gas pump at a local station.

Nancy, calm and supportive, drove us over to her home nearby so I could get away for a moment and call my family. She herself had been through the loss of a son; her six-month-old baby boy Jay had died of a rare disease several years before. She understood pain.

My mother, nearly four hundred miles away, was home alone when I told her the doctor's prognosis. The news was a chilling stun. In disbelief she tried to comfort me and told me not to stay by myself. How her heart must have ached for me as the reality of the situation sunk in.

Judy called Matt's sister, Lisa, who was away in school at Clemson University. She was going through some trying times herself, and the news of Matt's illness brought even more pain. Judy said Lisa began to cry hysterically. Clemson was only forty miles away, so one of her roommates would drive her home that night. She needed to be with her big brother.

As we made our way back to the doctor's office, we turned onto Main Street behind Larry's truck. He and Matt appeared to be laughing and cutting up. Though both men had a tendency to brush things off lightly, there must have been an anxiety about what awaited them at Dr. Smith's office. Surely they knew that something was terribly wrong.

"He's such a good-looking young man," his mother whispered proudly. Though unspoken, her thoughts were clear: *Why my son, God?* However heart-wrenching her inner thoughts and feelings, she remained composed and displayed a strength I had not seen in her before.

My thoughts blur as I recall getting out of the car, greeting Matt and Larry, and walking into the doctor's office. I remember trying to be strong, trying to hold back tears. There weren't enough chairs in the office, so Larry stood as Judy knelt beside Matt's chair. I sat on Matt's lap with my arms around his neck. I wanted to hold him close to me, to take him away to some distant place where we could be together and escape what was going on. But this was reality. This was the path that God had determined for us to walk. And I knew that we must accept it with His grace, His strength, His joy. Growing in the grace and knowledge of our Lord Jesus Christ through the past several years had prepared Matt to hear—and to accept—what was to come.

In his straightforward manner, Dr. Smith looked at Matt and repeated the piercing words he had spoken to us earlier.

"There's a possibility you might have lymphoma," he said calmly.

I can only imagine what Matt must have been feeling— maybe what we were all feeling, only magnified: disbelief, confusion, pain, numbness. Some time later he wrote, "The time right after that was a blur. I couldn't believe what was happening, for I had always been so healthy. It was like some bad dream which had found its way into my world of reality." Yet, as the bad dream was unfolding, he continued to make light of the situation by laughing and joking. I cried softly, wondering how he could hold in his feelings like that. Judy patted his hand and rubbed his head. Larry's face mirrored the depth of his concern.

A strong-willed, hard-working man, Larry Locke seldom displayed his feelings. His way of dealing with anger and discouragement was to go out to the woods, to chop down trees or plow a field. He probably could have chopped down entire forests as he listened to what the doctor was saying. How could this be happening to his son, his oldest boy? He was the one they had shared all the "firsts" with. Though he was no more loved than the other four children, Matt held a special place as the firstborn son.

Larry had no doubt treasured memories of watching his boy grow up, of the irreplaceable times they had spent together. But now something new was developing in their relationship. Though they did not agree on everything, they had a mutual respect for each other that deepened into a solid friendship. As an employer, Larry enjoyed having his son working for him and hoped that one day Matt would take over the business. He admired his son's high standards of moral conduct and the fact that Matt always stood firm for his beliefs. Matt's life had a big impact on his father. Less than two years before, Larry realized he did not have a personal relationship with Jesus. He publicly committed his life to the Lord, and God began changing his heart. Now his faith, still new, was being tested.

We left the doctor's office feeling empty, not knowing what to say or do next. They would have to do exploratory surgery to confirm our fears. Matt would be admitted to the hospital soon. But nothing was definite yet.

Matt and I went back to our house. This night would be one of the last few we would ever spend there. I couldn't stop crying, and I wanted him to cry with me. This was about his life, about our life together, and whether we would even have a chance for a life together. Whether it was because he wanted to be strong for everyone else like he always tried to be, or because the reality of the situation had not yet sunk in, or just because he didn't want to, Matt did not cry with me.

I was young, and in many ways an immature wife. I didn't know what else to do but cry and hold on to him. But then I asked him, "What can I do for you?" He knew he had my love, he knew he had my prayers. Yet I wanted to reach out to him in a way that nobody else possibly could.

"Be strong for me," he said simply.

From then on, I knew God would grant me the strength for Matt's sake. I could be strong for him. I could even be joyful for him, and make the days as bright as they possibly could be in this darkness.

By that evening, people all over town had heard about Matt's illness. It seemed like half the population of the neighboring towns of Honea Path and Belton were in some way kin to Matt Locke. From great-grandmothers to third cousins, from close friends to slight acquaintances, the people in the community were genuinely concerned.

Having lived in the area all his life, except for the years he was at college at Clemson and the summer he spent as a missionary at the Grand Canyon, Matt was well-known and highly regarded around town. The people began to pour their hearts out to us, sending food and money, running errands.

We went to Matt's parents' home for dinner that night. Someone had brought over some food, and though there was plenty to eat, nobody was hungry. The conversation seemed limited, almost forced. None of us knew quite what to say. Matt's three younger brothers were there: eighteen-year-old Ben, sixteen-year-old Russ, and fifteen-year-old David. Each had his own unique personality, but each of them was "all boy," too. They were tough on the surface, but their hearts were as sensitive as that of their big brother. They all looked up to Matt. He was their role model. But that evening, they kept whatever thoughts and feelings they had buried deep inside.

We all knew there was a battle ahead. However severe our previous fights had been in life, we'd weathered little compared to the approaching storm. At least I could say that was true for me. But I was confident of our Divine Resource. He said, "I Am all that you need." We had to trust Him to provide all that we needed.

Two days later I went back to work. I tried to relax, but I found it increasingly difficult to be my old self. I thought the day would never end, but around closing time, I got a call from Matt's mother.

"You might want to see if you can leave work a little early," she said. Her voice was strained. "We're going to go ahead and take Matt to the hospital."

Matt had been scheduled to enter the hospital early the next week. But that night, Thursday, he was weak and in severe pain. His jaundiced skin revealed a possible blockage of his bile duct. He needed medical attention, and next week was too far off.

As soon as I hung up the phone, I rushed out of the department store. The entire way home, I tried to push away the selfish thoughts going through my head. It was *my* place to be there with Matt. *I* should have been the one to say, "We're going to the hospital." I felt like an inadequate wife.

God would humble me. He would continue to strip away all that was not useful to Him—especially the selfish and prideful attitudes. He was what mattered; His work, His glory were far more important than my feelings and my presumed "place." And Matt was more important to me than myself. I needed to learn to let that show in my attitudes as well as my actions.

I spent that night in the hospital with Matt. I wanted to be with him every minute, no matter how draining that might be. He needed me. And I needed him.

Day and night, Matt was given shot after shot in an attempt to alleviate the pain—forty-seven of them in five days. His physical pain was tremendous, and so was the depth of emotional pain I felt for him. My husband, my best friend, my love was suffering right before my eyes, and I could do nothing to stop his pain. I felt helpless. I felt lost. I felt like my little part of the world was crumbling at my feet. Everything was falling so fast, and it seemed as though every ounce of physical, emotional, and spiritual strength was being drained from my body.

People consistently encouraged me to take a break, to get away from the hospital for a little while. Knowing I needed to be with my husband, I rarely took their advice. He needed me there, and I needed to be with him, to spend every minute I possibly could with him. He was such a precious gift to me, and I felt him slipping away. I was gripped by the fear of losing this wonderful man I had married just a few short weeks ago. Our life together was supposed to be just beginning. We had been looking forward to such a glorious future with each other. Was it possible now that we would never have the chance to grow old together?

God saw all of our pain, all of our frustration. He is not a distant God who doesn't know of our struggles. We knew that

He was right there with us, longing to hold us close to Himself, to dry our tears and bring peace to our troubled hearts. He provided the strength we needed to make it through those trying days.

The assurance of the Scriptures, the comfort of family and friends, the love of our Heavenly Father—all of these things were poured out to us during that time and in the months to follow. They brought us peace, even when we couldn't see through the darkness that lay ahead.

Matt's exploratory surgery was scheduled for Sunday, October 19. That Saturday was Clemson's homecoming, and the radio announcer for the game spoke of Matt and requested people to pray for "the former student body president who is battling with cancer." I appreciated the requests for prayer, but I was angry at this public announcement of "cancer." Even the doctors didn't know for sure. They had tried to give us every hope that the problem might only be a gall bladder disease, and I tried desperately to believe them.

Later that evening, Larry and I went to pick up a wedding present that had just arrived. My parents had bought us a washer, and Matt's parents gave us the matching dryer. They had been on order, and the store had called to let us know they were in. As Larry and I drove to the store, we talked of the possibility of Matt's illness being just a gall bladder disease.

"I believe they're gonna go in there and find out that's all it is," Larry said with determination. He was trying to convince me, I could tell.

"Me, too," I agreed, knowing deep inside that as much as I wanted to, I really didn't believe it at all.

The sunset was gloriously beautiful as we drove on in silence. Oh, if only this interruption in our lives could come to a close as beautifully as the day did!

Interruption? Not really. This was a piece of the puzzle, a part of the big picture God was unfolding, another step in our walk with Him. Most of the time it was hard for us to see through the darkness of the pain to the beauty of the picture, but we were learning that this is what faith is really all about ...and "the righteous shall live by faith."

My parents had driven from Alabama to be with me during the surgery, and with the three of us, Matt's family, and some close friends, we filled the hospital's tiny waiting room. The anxiety loomed like a dark cloud over that room. Silently, we were all praying, thinking, wondering. I tried to focus my thoughts on the Lord and on the good things He would do. In the moments prior to Matt's surgery, I had sat by his bedside in quietness. I felt a strange mixture of thankfulness, love, and sorrow for my husband, and I was suddenly overwhelmed with both joy and sadness. As Matt slept, I wrote down my thoughts.

> *Matt,*
>
> *As I sit beside you here in these moments before surgery, my heart overflows with love for you! To hear you breathing deeply and watch you as you sleep is such a blessing, especially after last night.*
>
> *I'm so thankful that I do not have to rely on my own strength to bring me through this ordeal. It hurts so much to see you suffer, to know that you're experiencing severe pain, and I can't do anything to relieve it. I feel so helpless.*

But our God is strong, and He is love and light. He has blessed us beyond measure and is working even now to fulfill His will for us.

I love you so much, Matt! Though my mind is cluttered and my thoughts are jumbled, there are a few things I'm sure of—my love for you and the fact that Jesus is my Lord, our Lord, and He loves us more than we know!

You are a precious treasure, and I know God's best will happen. I'm praying for you even as I write, and I can't wait to see what God is going to do.

Yours and His, Lisa

It is easy to say things, to say one trusts in God, to say one believes in His sovereignty and believes He is continually working for the good of those who love Him and are called according to His purpose. But to really know these things, to appropriate God's grace in believing, is something entirely different. We had to "reach out in steadfast faith and receive what belongs to us in our Lord Jesus Christ."

In his book *You Gotta Keep Dancin'*, Tim Hansel said, "All of our theology must eventually become biography. The constant challenge in this life we call Christian is the translation of all we believe to be true into our day-to-day lifestyle." Our theology was being translated and it was not easy, especially when I saw the doctor walking determinedly toward me through the waiting-room doors.

"The report's not good. There's some wild malignancy growing all through his abdomen. It looks like Burkitt's." His voice trailed off. Hot tears stung my face as I sobbed quietly. I wanted to run away and be alone. It seemed like Matt was already gone. Where was my faith? I couldn't stop the tears.

"Find rest, O my soul, in God alone; my hope comes from Him. He alone is my rock and my salvation; He is my fortress,

I shall not be shaken. My salvation and my honor depend on God; He is my mighty rock, my refuge. Trust in Him at all times, O people; pour out your hearts to Him, for God is our refuge" (Psalm 62:5-8).

The mood in the waiting room shifted abruptly from anxiety to sorrow. Hugs and words of encouragement offered little comfort. I dabbed my eyes and went to see Matt in the recovery room. On my way out the door, Matt's cousin Fredda stopped me. "You know you're going to have to tell him," she said. I knew, and I certainly didn't look forward to it.

Still drugged and incoherent, Matt was uncomfortable on the cold transport bed. Everything around us seemed cold and sterile. It felt so good to see him, no matter how he looked, to kiss his face and hold on to his hand. What a beautiful gift God had given me in my husband! Was He now to take this precious gift away?

With a shaky voice, I repeated what the doctor had told me. Matt seemed to hear me, but his face showed he didn't quite understand what I was saying. I held tightly to his hand as he was wheeled back to his room. For a moment neither of us spoke. Then he looked at me and asked me if he had cancer.

"Yes."

His face grimaced in pain as he received my answer. Later, he told me that he had suspected something this severe for quite a while. Why didn't he tell me? He never wanted to give anyone else cause for worry or fear.

We talked to the doctors several times over the next few days. Though they obviously cared about their patients, they answered our questions with an impersonal, businesslike manner. Prognosis: six weeks, maybe. Possible treatment: the National Cancer Institute in Bethesda, Maryland, a government-funded research hospital. How can we get him in? Doctor recommendation and acceptance into an existing program. And how long would that take? The admittance process to NCI usually takes two to three weeks. We didn't have two to three weeks.

But God knew our needs, and He was preparing the way for us long before we ever came to the crossroads. The doctor advised us to try any contacts we had to boost our chances of getting Matt into NCI, a branch of the National Institutes of Health. The hospital officials assured us that in the meantime, they would do everything they could. The day after Matt's surgery, we began calling.

The Lockes were not unfamiliar with NCI, nor with lymphoma. Matt's grandmother had a bout with the cancer, although it was a different type. She had been treated at NCI two years before. Her treatments of radiation and chemotherapy left her weakened, but ongoing checkups showed no signs of the disease. She had been in remission and feeling good for the last few years. We looked to her as an example of hope and miracles, daring to expect the same miracle for Matt.

The summer between his senior year in high school and his freshman year at Clemson, Matt had been a page for Strom Thurmond, the Republican senator from South Carolina. He lived at Senator Thurmond's home and worked closely with him. We knew that Senator Thurmond was a godly man, a solid politician, and an altruistic person. Someone contacted him.

Matt's father knew several men who worked in the state government. He would contact them. My dad called some friends in Alabama to see what they could do. We had a number of friends calling their government representatives in their counties or states. We had to try every possible avenue.

Early that morning, I called a friend whose father is a congressman. She would talk to her dad to see what he could do. As student body president at Clemson, Matt had met then-

Vice President of the United States George Bush at a university function. I called the Vice President's office and talked to his secretary. Meanwhile, our doctors had been in touch with NCI's doctors, and things were rolling.

Over the next few days we waited and prayed, and many waited and prayed with us. Hundreds of visitors came by the hospital to see Matt and to encourage us. Matt's room began to look like a combination of a florist and a post office. People were sending us their love. People were praying for us. People were anticipating the power of God.

Tuesday night we rejoiced at the good news: Matt had been accepted into the National Institutes of Health. We would be leaving the next day. Thanks to some folks at Clemson University and the generosity of a local corporation, a private plane and crew were provided to fly us up to National Airport on Wednesday afternoon.

Through the rush and confusion of those few days after surgery, Matt and I had little time for quiet, open talks. And it was so necessary. Sometimes all we could do was just look into each other's eyes. Mine usually clouded with tears; his communicated a mixture of love and sadness. I remember telling him I wanted us to do everything on our "one of these days" list before anything happened to him.

The nights were long and restless. I stayed in Matt's hospital room, and Fredda and Judy took turns spending the night with us. One night Matt was lying there in an unusually serene moment when his eyes suddenly welled up with tears. Worrying about his discomfort, Judy asked him what the matter was.

"God's so good to me," was his soft reply.

Only the gentle and loving ways of a gracious and compassionate God could cause one in so much pain to have an attitude like that, to see His goodness and mercy in spite of this present darkness. He was Matt's Light. He is still the Light. And He causes Himself to shine brightly in willing, humbled lives.

The community became genuinely interested in Matt's case. News reporters interviewed us and broadcast lengthy stories on the evening news. One journalist interviewed Matt in his hospital room the day before we left. Though jaundiced, weak, and in pain, Matt reflected a shining attitude.

"Lisa and I have been able to accept whatever the Lord has in store for us because all we want is His will and for Him to get the glory from whatever happens. But the biggest thing that gets to me is just to think about the goodness of the Lord and the people He's working through in this community."

We were truly thankful, and in spite of all the pain and sadness, I couldn't help feeling a little bit of adventure was up ahead. Our God is great and mighty in power; His understanding has no limits. I was so glad He understood me and my feelings that were both so different from and yet so similar to others who were close to Matt.

The morning we were to leave for Maryland, I went home for a few hours to rest and pack. It felt good to stretch out on our own bed, but I couldn't sleep. My thoughts were with Matt and all that was happening. My mind was spinning in a myriad of directions. The quiet time alone went by quickly, and before I knew it, I had to rush in order to make it back to the hospital on time. Our flight was scheduled to leave at two o'clock.

Some friends and family members promised their prayers and said goodbye at the hospital. Others followed the ambulance that carried Matt and me to the airport. A few reporters were there as well. Louise Ervin, editor of the *Anderson Independent-Mail* had watched Matt grow up. She had written several articles about him in the past—his prize dairy heifer, his election as state student council president in high school, his terms as student body president in high school and college.

When this crisis arose, she was on hand to capture the courageous struggle of a young man the entire community admired.

"Promising Future Becomes Fight for Life," read the big, bold headline of the newspaper's front-page story. The subhead gave further details: "CU Graduate Looks to God, Caring Friends for Courage to Battle Cancer." A picture of Matt, bright-eyed with a serious smile, ran beside the article. It wasn't one of my favorite pictures of my husband. It didn't capture his bubbly personality, the lively aura that was so much a part of Matt. Understandably, he didn't feel quite that lively right now, but his attitude was certainly one of positive expectancy and hope.

"This is an opportunity to be a witness for Christ," Matt was quoted in the article. "Lisa and I know it is all in God's hands and we are trusting Him. Whatever happens, we want to bring glory to Him."

And so that was our hope—to bring glory to Jesus Christ. "And whatever you do, whether in word or deed, do all in the name of the Lord Jesus, giving thanks to God the Father through Him."

Our hopes were as bright as the sky above as we boarded the lear jet. But the light breeze couldn't blow away the tension that was in the air. Some of the faces behind us seemed to wonder if they would ever see Matt again. Yet none of us is promised a tomorrow. Numerous things could have happened to prevent us from seeing one another again on this earth—a plane crash, a storm, or (blessed hope!) Jesus' return. We were assured of our place in God's kingdom, so no matter what might happen to us, we were "more than conquerors through Him who loved us." Was God allowing us this opportunity to let others know His truth, His love? I wondered, but I didn't see it clearly at the start.

Initially, my thoughts about our circumstances were puzzled, questioning, even defiant. *Why, God? You haven't even given us a chance to serve You together. We have so much potential. We have willing hearts. We really want to serve You. Couldn't You use us better as a team, working side by side for You?*

Little by little, He opened my eyes to see more clearly. Not fully understanding, yet seeing enough to trust and obey, I realized that He *was* giving us a wonderful and mysterious chance to serve Him together in a unique and beautiful way. Through our love for Him and our love for each other, we could face this thing with joy in our hearts even though we had tears in our eyes.

The flight was short and smooth. Under different circumstances, it would have been quite enjoyable. With the load of luggage we had packed, we barely had room to squeeze in both sets of parents and Fredda.

Fredda was a blessing to have with us. As a nurse, she knew just what to do to make Matt more comfortable, to ease his difficulty in breathing. It was not easy for Matt to be restful while he was lying on a stretcher bridged over some seats. But at last, the wheels of the plane touched down at busy National Airport in Washington, D.C.

Matt and I said hurried but affectionate goodbyes to our fathers and to Fredda; they would be returning on the plane to South Carolina. Our mothers would be staying with us for a little while, and we were to meet them at the National Institutes of Health, a twenty-five minute drive from the airport. As we climbed into the ambulance, I focused my attention on getting to the hospital and finding some relief for Matt. The thought of our mothers back at the airport didn't even occur to me.

"We're almost there. We're almost there." The emergency medical technician who rode in the back of the ambulance with us kept assuring us the ride would not be long.

We turned off the beltway through a tailored neighborhood. Ahead were immaculately sculptured grounds looking like a college campus. As we turned into a driveway leading through the grounds, we saw fourteen stories of dark glass looming ahead. The National Institutes of Health. What was behind those walls of glass?

I felt as though I were made from walls of glass myself. And someone, somewhere, was throwing stones at me.

We rolled Matt through the double doors of the front entrance. While I stopped at the admitting desk to fill out the paperwork, the EMT crew took Matt to his room. I wanted to go with my husband. I felt peaceful and secure when I was holding his hand. So I rushed through the admittance papers as quickly as I could and hurried up to the thirteenth floor. Even the elevator ride was much too long for me.

Matt's room was right across from the nurses' station and close to the ice machine, quite a convenience since he was on a strict diet of ice chips for the time being. We met several of the attending nurses and doctors, and Matt's doctor said he would speak with us again that evening when our mothers arrived. At that time he would answer any and every question we had.

There was a unique attitude among the staff there. They were friendly, yes, and certainly professional. But there was something deeper that allowed us to get close to them, for them to get close to us. They were full of compassion and concern for us, even though we had just met. In situations like ours, in times of crisis, people tend to cut through the polite veneer and reach straight to the heart. We were all going through this ordeal together, working together, growing together.

One of Matt's primary nurses was a very capable woman named Sandy. She was an experienced oncology nurse who had seen much pain and suffering over the past twelve years at NIH. We could see it in her eyes. Though her voice was soft and tender, she spoke with knowledge and authority. And her gentle, peaceful manner made us feel relaxed and comfortable in her presence.

Later that night, we met Matt's other primary nurse, Eileen. A lively Irish, Eileen had energy and humor to go along with her adept nursing skills. She was our age, and while Sandy would become more of a mother figure to us, Eileen was to become our buddy. But on that first day, we were just getting acquainted.

The nurses checked on us every few minutes for the first hour or so, getting Matt settled, making sure he was comfortable, telling us a little of what was going on. I appreciated all they were doing, but I longed to be alone with Matt, just for a little while.

As I reflected on the past week, I thought about how little time we had been alone together. Ever since the surgery, it seemed that someone else was always in the room with us. Matt and I had not had a chance to really talk about what was happening, to express what we were both feeling so deeply. So many visitors, so many plants and flowers, so many cards, not enough time or space. It was as though Matt and I had been crowded out of each other's lives by all the concerned well-wishers.

Here in Maryland, we would finally have some space to just be together. Still, we had a hard time communicating what was inside. Was the cut too deep to bleed freely? Were we afraid to pour out our fears before each other? Though we didn't talk much of our fears, there would never be too many "I love you's" or other expressions that indicated that our love for each other was steadfastly growing and deepening.

Our hearts were heavy because of Matt's illness, but there was still room for comic relief. Our mothers made it to the hospital with yet another story to tell of country people in the big city. My mother was no stranger to urban America, but Judy Locke had spent her entire life in Honea Path, South Carolina—a place where someone from Maryland is considered a "foreigner."

With eight suitcases and several large bags, the two women somehow made their way through the airport. Rubbing shoulders with all those government officials carrying impressive-looking briefcases and making their way past pinstripe-clad businesswomen, Judy and my mother precariously maneuvered our belongings into the taxi line. They were met by arguing, foreign taxi drivers trying to grab our bags from each other and get more business. The driver next in line didn't have enough room for all the luggage, but he began to load his trunk anyway. A station wagon sat second in line, and our mothers hailed that driver as they began to unload our things from the first taxi. Much to the dismay of the first driver, they finally got everything loaded into the vehicle behind him and were soon headed toward Bethesda, across the Potomac River.

A wild ride to the motel left them a bit shaken, but after checking in and dropping off the luggage, they made it to NIH and asked where they could find us. It seems everyone in that hospital knew about Matt Locke, and the front desk clerks told our mothers that there was so much political interest in this patient that they had expected to see them arrive by limousine. The beat-up taxi was a far cry from a limo, but it brought them safely to us. The desk clerks directed them to the elevator leading to the patient units. We were glad they had finally arrived so we could hear what the doctor had to say. We had made it to NIH. Now what?

<hr>

Dr. Stevenson was a dedicated physician, committed to a partnership with his patients; they work together to combat diseases. He was always willing to listen or answer our questions, always wanting the best treatment as soon as possible. We found Dr. Stevenson to be caring and loyal. His eyes, though hidden behind the shaded lenses of his glasses, reflected his concern and commitment. His stamina and appearance made him look much younger than his late thirties.

Dr. Stevenson spent several hours with us informing us of the seriousness of Matt's condition, the severity of the treatments, and the hoped-for results. I jotted down some notes as he talked. *Diffuse undifferentiated lymphoma, Burkitt's type. Very serious, but very treatable. Therapy about eight months. Tumor confined to belly. Lymph node cells that have "gone astray."* Chemotherapy and radiation were in order. Matt would have to get a lot sicker before he would begin to get better. That was chemotherapy. Treatments were scheduled to begin the next day.

Matt seemed to sleep better that night. I was thankful for his rest—he seemed to get so little of it these days. The pull-out chair which served as my bed in his hospital room did not offer me much comfort—neither did the fact that the nurses had to check on him repeatedly throughout the night. Yet I couldn't even think about being anywhere other than by my husband's side. I wanted so much to look into his mind, to see what was going on in there. What was he thinking? He must have been emotionally, physically, and spiritually drained. I was.

"But those who hope in the Lord will renew their strength. They will soar on wings like eagles; they will run and not grow weary, they will walk and not be faint" (Isaiah 40:31). His hope, our hope, was in the Lord. And Jesus said, "Come to me, all you who are weary and burdened, and I will give you rest. Take my yoke upon you and learn from me, for I am gentle and humble in heart, and you will find rest for your souls. For my yoke is easy and my burden is light" (Matthew 11:28-30). Matt needed rest. I needed rest. We needed Jesus...and He was with us.

Though we knew we could rest in God's care for us, and we knew that only through Him could we experience peace of heart and mind, there was no time for peace and rest, at least not physically. Our first full day at NCI was full indeed: EKGs, a myelogram, x-rays, scans, and more doctors. Andrea was Matt's nurse for the day, and she got a lot of exercise wheeling his portable bed around the maze of corridors as he went from test to test. Like Eileen, Andrea was our age, and she was fairly new on the thirteenth floor. Her pleasant smile was an encouragement to us.

I was not permitted to accompany Matt to all of his various tests, so I passed the hours looking over our temporary home. Later that morning, I sat in one of the many waiting rooms and began another letter.

October 23

Matt,

I just finished eating and "touring" a small part of this colossal place. I wanted so much to stay with you and hold your hand and be beside you. But it's probably better that I had to leave the room—I can't handle watching you hurt, grimacing in pain. They're putting you through so much today.

After his last test I rejoined Matt, and as we wheeled in the direction of the elevator in the radiation therapy unit, we saw some familiar faces coming toward us. Our mothers were there, but so were a crowd of others. One man in a bright red sweater stood out, and I immediately recognized the husky, bearded man. His eyes twinkled behind his glasses, and his smile was no less bright. It was John, the former Baptist campus minister at Clemson, and he had driven up from Richmond, Virginia, to see us.

Dr. Bill Atchley and his wife greeted us with friendly smiles and firm handshakes. Dr. Atchley was the former president of Clemson University, and after he left Clemson, he and his wife had moved to McLean, Virginia. The day before, he had been thinking of an old friend and decided to give him a call. This friend was the same man who provided the plane for us to fly to NCI. He told the Atchleys of our circumstances, and they came to give us their support.

Matt had met the Atchleys at the beginning of his term as student body president at Clemson. We never had the opportunity to really get to know them, so we were touched by the warmth of their embraces. They had brought us food and magazines. And since our mothers were at the mercy of the taxi drivers, the Atchleys loaned us one of their cars for several weeks. In the months to come, we would spend a lot more time with them. More precious gifts from God. We were thankful.

The hellos were brief, as Matt was scheduled for his first treatment soon. At four o'clock, he was given "pre-medication" to cause drowsiness and curb some of the nausea that the treatment was certain to cause. For the first time in days, Matt was sleeping serenely, his chest rising and falling with each deep breath. He slept through his first chemotherapy treatment—the most crucial—and continued his restful slumber well into the night. His first treatment had gone beautifully.

Twelve hours later, Matt was awake and in good spirits. He was bright and alert, and asked if I would like to read him some of the mail he had received at the hospital back in Anderson.

"Matt, it's four o'clock in the morning!"

He couldn't believe he had slept that long. We laughed. He seemed to feel better than he had in days.

Though he didn't talk much about what was going on inside him, Matt wrote some of his innermost thoughts on paper a few days after we arrived in Bethesda.

Today is Saturday and I spent almost all of it in bed, as I have this past week. The reason is that I am sick (physically). It seems like only yesterday that I was one of the most healthy people around. As far as sports went, my limits were where my interests stopped. I was proud of the strong body and physique that I possessed, but now that has all changed.

It all happened so fast. First I noticed an inability to get a deep breath. I didn't pay much attention to that. Then I developed pain in my abdominal region and back and after a few days of not being able to bear it, I went to the doctor. At first he thought maybe it was just tension, then an ulcer. I got no relief being treated for either. Then I had some tests run. They found a mass in my stomach, then did exploratory surgery on Sunday, October 19th. They found it was Burkitt's lymphoma, cancer.

Now I'm at Bethesda, Maryland, undergoing some of the roughest cancer treatment they have, but it seems to be working so far. I've got to admit I am scared, but I know the Lord is with me.

Most of our fears are rooted in things mysterious to us, the anticipation of the unwanted, the uncertainty of the unknown. Matt and I had to learn to trust God with those things if we were ever to find joy in our present circumstances. I thought back to when we first began dating, when Matt had written to me some beautiful words of wisdom:

I don't know about you, but I often find myself thinking about the future. I sometimes face the future with fear and many times with joy, but I've come to realize that the future should not even concern me now. It is something I do not understand and can do nothing about now, but the present is a different story. The good Lord offers us all the present, so let us put our all into now and trust the future with all of its mystery to Him.

This is the day that the Lord has made—can we rejoice and be glad in it? We *will* rejoice and be glad in it!

Although our journals had been our close companions for many years, neither Matt nor I made regular entries during those days we were facing such hardship. We both made entries, my first since we arrived in Maryland, on the same day.

October 29

We've been in Maryland for a week now, and it seems like months. Far away from home, yet home when we're together. Sometimes there is tension, sometimes sadness, yet always a tender closeness, a touching bond—the wanting to hold each other so close and never let go, never say goodbye.

We spent our first night away from each other since we've been married, and it seemed so long. It was strange not to feel the warmth of his body beside me, or, as it has been these past two weeks in the hospital, to have him an arm's reach away. I didn't rest well.

Tonight I will try to sleep through the night. It's my first night in a real bed in a few weeks.

Matt wrote his thoughts that night, too.

Well, I've been here exactly 1 week now. Things are going pretty good, considering all that is going on. I've already endured several treatments of chemotherapy and radiation...I've also gotten sick several times from all they have given me, but I can put up with the temporary for the long-term benefits. I just can't wait until all of this is over with and we can get back to life as normal. Or will life ever really be back to normal again?

I sometimes lie and wonder what life will be like after this incident. It could change many things. Especially my life plans may be changed. Now it's like going for those things that always seemed important to me are things that I need to go for now.

I think what I would really like to do is to travel around speaking, and letting people know about God's goodness. I'm tired of feeling sorry for myself. I've got it made. Everything is going my way and I've encountered only a temporary setback.

Lord, I'm going to give this thing all that I have, and I trust You to provide all that I need.

It's a shocking realization to discover the truth that our lives are beyond our control. We cannot go beyond the limits God has ordained for us. "Many are the plans in a man's heart, but it is the Lord's purpose that prevails" (Proverbs 19:21). Often we do not understand His purposes. But we don't always have to understand. In submissive obedience to Him, we are able to find joy, security, peace, real love—all we really long for deep down inside—no matter what the circumstances. It is our relationship to a perfect, sovereign God that is able to sustain us through times of trial and crisis.

Through our hurt, we knew we could trust the Lord. Through our doubt and fears, we trusted Him. Through our short-sighted vision, through our suffering, we trusted Him. Matt was experiencing a great deal of physical pain, but that seemed secondary to the matters and feelings laying heavy on his heart. Yet he trusted the Lord. His body was plagued with nausea, fatigue, weakness, and numerous side effects from the drugs and treatments. But his spirit glowed with a radiant joy.

The hospital staff soon found out that we had been married for only a few months. Realizing the importance of maintaining intimacy, especially through this time when we needed each other so much, they made some special arrangements for us. One of the nurses made a "Do Not Disturb" sign for us to hang on the door when we wanted to be alone. Of course there were a few stipulations for its use. Whenever we wanted complete privacy, we had to first check with the staff to make sure Matt had no treatments or tests scheduled. Then, if we put out the sign, *no one* was allowed to bother us unless it was an extreme emergency. On several occasions, nurses, friends, even doctors refrained from knocking on the door because of the sign.

Matt and I enjoyed those times behind closed doors with our handy "Do Not Disturb" sign. One particular night with the sign securely on the door, we held each other close in the small hospital bed. The lights were low, the room was quiet, and Matt was feeling energetic.

As we held each other in a passionate embrace, just enjoying the rare beauty of being alone together, Matt's IV pump machine began to ring loudly. One of the nurses would have to come reprogram it. Like a flash of lightning, I jumped out of bed, grabbed my clothes, and was dressed in less than fifteen seconds. Matt was laughing hysterically. It was so good to see him laugh. We relished that laughter together. Minutes later, a nurse was at the door.

"Yes, you may come in now." I knew I must be blushing.

When she left, we went right back to where we had been before the interruption. And we didn't let that incident keep us from making good use of the sign.

Matt had a beautiful spirit, and the nurses and doctors loved him. People were drawn to him because of his good nature and the love that flowed from his life. Even on the "bad days" he could smile. But the nausea threatened to get him at the best of times.

For a while I kept a log of every drug Matt received, every treatment he went through, every new action that occurred. I found notes on when he took his first shower, when he began different diets, even when he first passed gas after surgery. It was important to me to keep up with every little thing my husband was going through. I so wanted to be a part of every area in his life—even his suffering.

October 30

Matt had a miserable day today—after radiation he threw up. After chemo he threw up four times. I hate to see him go through all this, but I know he must—to get better. I met Peter today, and Ted, too. They room next door to each other on the opposite side of the hall. Both of them were very friendly.

I hope Matt sleeps well—he was in a deep sleep when we left him.

Thank You, Lord, for trials.

In addition to the adjustments of dealing with Matt's illness and all the changes in our lives resulting from that, we were still adjusting to a new marriage. The adjustments were not always easy.

October 31

Today was a long day. Matt felt good most of the day, but all he wanted to do was watch television. He snapped at me several times, but was cheery and pleasant with the nurses and everyone else

It hurts when he does that, but I know his love is constant, for You have given him a love for me. God, teach me more about this thing called marriage and this thing called love that You are! I love You!

Though I wanted my heart to be after God's own heart, to be the best wife for my husband, my perspective was often clouded by my own expectations and how I wanted things to be. I wanted Matt to be open with me about all of his feelings and pain. I wanted him to feel free to be weak with me. I wanted him to share the deepest parts of himself with me.

November 1

Matt had an okay day—nothing seems to help him get over that nauseous feeling. He's not only hurting physically, he seems to be in so much emotional pain. He is holding so much in—I wish he would cry with me just once.

Because of the way Matt was brought up, he didn't cry much. The few times I saw him cry were for others' pain, sometimes when he spoke before groups about the Lord's goodness and mercy, and in a few deeply emotional prayer times. Rarely did he cry to release his own pain, his own inner hurts. Often I prayed for God to help me understand him and love him in the ways he needed to be loved.

November 2

Lord Jesus, comfort Matt—become really real to him during this time. Help me to reach out to him and touch him with Your love and power. I love You!

Were my expectations of Matt and myself too high? We had a solid relationship built on the Rock, but our lives were definitely not "normal." He could no longer support us and care for me the way he wanted to, and this led to feelings of guilt and inadequacy. What could I do to keep him from feeling this way? I wanted so much to reach inside him and bring out all the pain and hurt. I wanted to be a comfort to him. Sometimes only Jesus can do that. I had to trust Him.

Without our realizing it, the Lord was using us in each other's lives in a strong way. We began to see the importance of letting each other know the value of "us, together." Matt penned a beautiful love letter to express such feelings:

Dearest Sweetheart,

I haven't been much at writing love notes to you over the past few weeks. I've been focusing my mind too much on what has been going on, and that does neither of us any good. I feel like I've shirked some in my responsibility to be all that I should for you. I don't know what I would do without you. I can't even imagine my life absent from the beauty which you bring to it.

You have been all that I've needed in this time of trial. You have always been there with your smile or words of encouragement, even sometimes when it was extremely difficult for you to do so. You have spent many sleepless nights suffering through my pain with me, yet you never complained. You were the poor soul who always got to see what the real Matt Locke is like, and amazingly, you continue to love me just the same.

Just being without you for a short while makes me realize how much I need and rely on you. You are truly a part of me that I cannot do without. I love you with all of my heart. Just please be patient with me if I sometimes don't feel too loving over the next few weeks. What we have to go through is tough, but I know we can make it.

Love forever, Matt

P.S. I hope you'll love me as much when I'm bald!

Gracious and loving God. Gracious and loving Matt. I knew that I had been chosen to receive this love from God. He had saved me; He was transforming me; He continued to prepare me for this bonding together of our hearts and our minds through marriage and through the trials. God was blessing me richly through Matt's love and devotion to me. *Thank you, God. Thank you, Matt.*

Because NIH is a government-funded institute, we did not have to pay for any of Matt's hospital care—the room, drugs, tests, therapies, and treatment were all provided for. In addition, many of the local residents opened up their homes to families of NIH patients, so our mothers rented a room in the home of a friendly and lively lady named Mrs. Eddy.

Active in the community for many years, Mrs. Eddy enjoyed helping people, like providing temporary living quarters at low rent. She lived about three miles from the hospital and had plenty of space.

Matt's condition was beginning to improve with the treatment, and after a week of staying with him in his room, the hospital staff told me I needed to find a place to stay, so I could be comfortable and get more rest. I didn't like the idea at all. I wanted to be with Matt every single minute. But I knew it was hospital regulations and would be best in the long run. So I decided to join our mothers at Mrs. Eddy's.

To keep him company at night, Matt kept a teddy bear with him which had been given to us by some friends before we left South Carolina. We named it "Burkie" after Matt's disease, Burkitt's lymphoma. The nurses really got a kick out of that. And though it was in no way a sufficient substitute for me, Burkie reminded Matt every night of the prayers and support of our friends. We needed reminders, especially through the rough roads ahead.

The protocol designed to treat cancers such as lymphoma was extremely rigorous. The toxic chemicals proved to be an insult to the body, harming the bone marrow, weakening the body's natural immune system. In the first twenty-eight-day cycle of Matt's treatments, he would receive at least six different drugs on the first, fourth, eighth, fifteenth, and twenty-second days. In addition, he had to undergo several spinal taps and twelve treatments of radiation to the brain as a preventive measure.

Within weeks of Matt's initial treatment, his condition began to improve. As the football-sized tumor rapidly responded to the chemotherapy, the severe pain in his back and abdomen decreased greatly. It had become so much a part of his daily life that he almost didn't remember what it was like not to be in constant pain.

The first time Matt was able to go out on a pass away from the hospital was certainly a scary adventure. Having to leave the security of an entourage of nurses, readily available medication, and a reasonably comfortable hospital bed made Matt a bit nervous. Still, we tried to enjoy ourselves as much as possible. I captured our short vacation in my journal that night.

November 4

Matt was able to go out on pass today. After his IG-IV infusion and a shower, we left the hospital around four o'clock. We stopped by the store and our moms went in while we waited in the car. We saw a car with a Clemson sticker and wrote them a note.

When we got back to Mrs. Eddy's we all ate some leftovers from food the Atchleys brought. Matt and I laid down on my bed, then decided to go to a motel. He'd gotten sick twice, but he wanted to stay out. We had a great time for a while. Then he started getting sick a lot about 11:45, and we decided we better go back to the hospital. He got sick a few more times after that, and they finally gave him some medicine to help him rest through the night. But I didn't sleep very well.

Though Matt was getting better in one sense, he was getting worse in another. In the first two months of treatment, I watched him lose fifty pounds, his beautiful thick hair, his strength, and his Charles Atlas physique. He also lost some of the feeling in his fingertips, and it became difficult for him to write. His voice became shaky and raspy, making it nearly impossible for him to sing, something he had always loved to do. Many of the things that he had taken for granted, many of the things that had been such an integral part of his life, were slipping from his grasp.

Yet one thing he never lost was his faith in Christ Jesus. I don't know if Matt thought much about those verses which Paul wrote to the church at Philippi, but every time I read them, I thought of him: "But whatever was to my profit I now consider loss for the sake of Christ. What is more, I consider everything a loss compared to the surpassing greatness of knowing Christ Jesus my Lord, for whose sake I have lost all things. I consider them rubbish, that I may gain Christ..." (Philippians 3:7-8).

What else is there in this life? What else is there to live for? I have seen others grope in darkness, grasping at anything to keep them from sinking, trying to hold on to lies and fantasies and selfish dreams, hoping they'll find what they need to get through another day. I've watched people stumble all over the truth, questioning the meaning of life, looking all around them at the things of the earth instead of searching for the only One who holds the answers. And I continually ask myself, *How can anyone really live without Jesus?* I don't mean merely existing, getting by, going through the motions of living. I mean abundant life. How can anyone *really* live without Jesus?

As I lived around patients and people in pain, I wondered even more, *How can anyone make it through this without Him?* Day after day in the hospital, bodies weakened in every way, needles, IVs, nurses, doctors—and the only hope is the hope that each allows himself to have. Without Jesus there would be no reason, no purpose, no hope or comfort or joy—no real life and no real love.

Yet we serve a sovereign God who is continually working all things for the good of those who love Him, those who are called according to His purpose. We knew that we were called according to His purpose, and it brought joy to see the many ways He was working through our experience.

God was touching people's hearts, turning their faces toward Him, calling people to prayer. So many friends and acquaintances told us about the impact our experience was having on their lives. Churches all over South Carolina, in Alabama, and in other parts of the country committed to pray for us. People's prayer lives deepened; they came before a caring and loving God—the Great Physician—with requests for Matt's healing, for comfort and strength for us both; they were open to the Spirit's leading in their praise, their thanksgiving, their confession, and their intercession.

Small groups on Clemson's campus began meeting for prayer. They were, as a result, drawn closer together as a body of believers united in a common purpose. People began to see so very clearly the awesome power of prayer. And no one saw it better than Matt and I did. We had claimed a verse for ourselves: "And my God will meet all your needs according to His glorious riches in Christ Jesus." True to His promise, God was meeting all our needs.

During one of our quiet afternoons together, Matt and I made a list of who God is to us, and a separate list of the things we were thankful for at this time. The lists were by no means exhaustive, but we wanted to "count it all joy" (James 1:2). We thought a conscious effort to consider all the Lord had done for us would be helpful in making us realize His blessings through this time of pain. So we decided to actually count our blessings.

> *<u>Who God is to us</u>: friend, counselor, comforter, Father, provider, understanding, gives room and encouragement to grow, sensitive, gentle, caring, almighty, omnipotent, everywhere, gives purpose, beauty, life!*
>
> *<u>Our thanksgivings</u>: life, love, Matt & Lisa, families, Jesus, time together, friends, churches, doctors and nurses, NIH, cancer treatment, generosity of people everywhere, prayer, answers to prayer, suffering, trials, adversity, Clemson, education, sex!*

We were thankful to know the Giver of every good and perfect thing; He touched us in so many ways. We saw His love in our families, through their commitment and support. We saw His love in the encouragement of friends and people we barely knew at all. We saw His love in the care and concern of the hospital staff. We were showered with love.

Every day, Matt received flowers, balloons, cards, and letters. Some days we received more than fifty pieces of mail, many from people we didn't even know, people who had heard about our situation and wanted to show their concern. We even received packages from elementary school classes, homemade cards and colored pictures, computer-printed banners. Just as Matt had reached out to people, always giving so freely of himself, people were reciprocating the love and concern. And the surprises continued to come.

Several Clemson graduates were living in the Washington, D.C., area and we met many of them. Casual acquaintances from school days became close friends. One such friend, Ray, had run against Matt for student body president at Clemson. Their relationship at the time was one of "political friendliness." It seemed that throughout the race, Ray tried fervently to outclass Matt. As I remember it, the election was charged with highly competitive attitudes and political scheming. Though I had a biased opinion, I felt "the opponent" was trying to put on a better show to bring in the votes. Yet Matt in his easygoing, friendly style had the edge—he had committed the election to the Lord.

The results of the election spoke loud and clear. With the largest voter turnout Clemson had seen in years, Matt received 62 percent of the student body's vote.

Though he believed God put him in the position of student body president, he really didn't know what to expect. About a month into the fall term, Matt wrote in his journal about his new "job."

September 26, 1985

Boy, this has been one busy semester. Sometimes, well, all of the time, I feel I'm majoring more in student government than anything. I end up going from one meeting to another, but inside I still don't feel I've accomplished what I set out to do. What is it that I set out to do?

Most of all, I wanted to make a difference. I wanted to work in lives. I want to make people realize what real living is all about. Jesus provides so much to a life, so much to my life. So first and foremost, I want Christ to be seen through me.

Second, and right along with this, I want to help people. It's great being able to get on the phone with someone and remedy a problem within a matter of moments.

Third, I want to do my best to make Clemson University as great a university as I possibly can. I want people from all over to really desire to get into Clemson because it is one of the best educational institutions around.

Why did I run for student body president? Why do I always have to get involved? The reason is the Lord has given me an overwhelming desire to achieve and even to overachieve. I feel that too often when I reach that goal I was searching for, I don't know what to do then.

Lord, help me to be more committed to You. Help me to be alive in You.

Love, Matt

Whatever competitive feelings had existed during the election disappeared when Ray found out about Matt's illness. As a medical student, Ray was interested in finding out more about Matt's lymphoma and its treatments; as a friend, Ray was interested in finding out about Matt's personal, emotional, and spiritual well-being.

Through the months of Matt's treatment, Ray was faithful to call or to come by for a visit. He usually brought us a newspaper or a puzzle, and he always brought us his concern and genuine friendship.

The Lord continued to bring a variety of people into our lives to minister to us, and for us to minister to in a unique way. One afternoon as Matt dozed off under the influence of his pre-medication for yet another chemo treatment, a beautiful girl with dark hair, bright blue eyes, and a radiant smile stood in the doorway of the hospital room. I felt like I knew her even as she introduced herself, a friend of a friend of a friend. Gwen was a close friend of Matt's; Mary Ann was a close friend of Gwen's; Jenné was a close friend of Mary Ann's. Jenné would become a close friend of ours, too.

When she walked into the room, I immediately sensed a bond with her. I felt as though we had known each other for years. She radiated a special warmth, an unselfish love that reached out through her eyes, her smile, her words. She stayed for several hours, and I felt a twinge of sadness when she stood to leave. Before she left she asked sincerely, "What can I pray about for you?"

Jenné, our new God-sent friend, someone to laugh with, to cry with, to share late-night talks and crazy moments with, someone to pray with. Without hesitation, Jenné invited me to come stay with her and her roommates while Matt was in the hospital. I wouldn't have to pay any rent; they wanted me to live with them. *Thank you, Lord Jesus, for Your blessings.*

As one of the side effects of the chemotherapy, Matt's healthy, sandy-colored hair began to fall out. I remember the day he began pulling it out in big clumps. All I wrote in my journal was: *Matt's fever was down—temp normal most of the day— blood pressure still low—hair started coming out.*

Matt expressed much deeper thoughts than mine that day.

November 8

I lay here wondering what I will tell people about my situation once I am clear of it, once it's all just a memory preserved by some surgical scars. What will I tell people when they ask me how we made it through? I guess I would have to say God and God alone. But have I really allowed God to show forth His full power in me? I must say, I think not. I read my Bible and pray a little now and then. That isn't the mind of Christ; that's the mind of Matt giving the Lord an invitation to come along.

Lord, I really want to know You and Your will for my life. I want to stop playing at all of this and get serious at being a Christian. Lord, I really need You to lean on.

I've been thinking far too much here lately about money, and having a lot, but that's not where it's at. Lord, guide my thoughts and my actions.

Psalm 121: "I lift my eyes to the hills—where does my help come from? My help comes from the Lord, the Maker of heaven and earth. He will not let your foot slip—He who watches over Israel will neither slumber nor sleep. The Lord watches over you—the Lord is your shade at your right hand; the sun will not harm you by day, nor the moon by night. The Lord will keep you from all harm—He will watch over your life; the Lord will watch over your coming and going both now and forevermore."

How many of us have had thoughts similar to those of Matt? Our minds giving the Lord an invitation to join us in our ways of thinking. Playing at being a Christian. Saying all the right things. Doing everything we're supposed to do. But never fully being all God desires—being fully His.

"Seek the Lord while He may be found; call on Him while He is near. Let the wicked forsake his way and the evil man his thoughts. Let him turn to the Lord, and He will have mercy on him, and to our God, for He will freely pardon. 'For my thoughts are not your thoughts, neither are your ways my ways,' declares the Lord. 'As the heavens are higher than the earth, so are my ways higher than your ways and my thoughts than your thoughts'" (Isaiah 55:6-9).

"But seek first His kingdom and His righteousness, and all these things will be given to you as well" (Matthew 6:33).

"Apart from me you can do nothing" (John 15:5).

Inner struggles caused us to look at Jesus, but our sincere questions seemed to take priority on our prayer agendas. *Yes, Lord, but why this? Do we have to go through this fire? Where is the other side of this valley?*

Through the fire, the Lord was refining us, shaping us, polishing us to reflect His light a little bit better.

"Whatever it takes," Matt had prayed. Did he really mean that? Did I have the same attitude of heart? *Yes, Lord. Whatever it takes.*

Though my feelings were deep and sometimes sharp, I often lacked the physical and emotional energy to write about what was going on inside. I found myself recording external events, activities, things—maybe just to write about something, anything, other than what I was feeling.

November 9

We had a nice day together—Judy went out with some friends for dinner and Mom stayed at Mrs. Eddy's for a while, so we had a little time alone.

Bob went to church with Judy and me. He's a unique character. A woman conducted the service, and it was different. I miss church, God. I miss worshiping with a family of believers. Show me my place, God.

There's so much inside bursting to come out, but I don't have the words or the energy to write any longer. I'll read instead. Thank You, good Lord, for all the blessings!

November 10

Charlie (another patient) passed away this morning—I wish he would've had a few good days before he went home to You, God. Thank You that he's not suffering any more.

Lord, comfort Matt. Be real to him now. Help him to open his heart and mind to You, to love You.

November 11

Matt and I took a bath together today. It was fun! Lord, every time I look at him I fall in love with him all over again—and it makes me love You even more for sharing him with me. What a precious gift.

We owe You so much. Help us. Show us how to yield to You, almighty God! I love You.

November 12

God, show me how I need to be used here. There are so many people with so many needs. My first responsibility is to You, then to Matt.

We watched a couple of movies tonight. But Matt is always so groggy when they give him that medicine.

Take care of him, Lord. I love him! But I know that all my love is but a splash of water compared to Your love for him.

November 13

Thank You for Your perfect example of how to love, Lord Jesus. Remind me that love is patient and kind and unselfish—never jealous or boastful or proud or rude, yet love bears all things, believes all things, endures all things. Your love never fails—thank You for loving me!

Matt's having a rough day. He had a few reactions to one of his drugs to counteract nausea. His whole body was tense and shaky, and his face contorted. It lasted about thirty minutes. He's relaxing now—about to get a new IV because he pulled the other one out during the second reaction—the second reaction was a lot less severe. He hasn't had a very good day.

He stayed still and rested after chemo. Hooray—his last treatment of the first cycle and his last radiation therapy were today! Thank You, God, for getting us through it all.

November 14

A much better day for Matt—a bunch of guys came by and brought him a Clemson cap and an autographed football. The Athletic Department has been so good to us.

My family came tonight—even Joe and Sandy were here. They stayed with me while Mom and Dad went to a motel. Matt only got sick a few times. Doctor's rounds—they said he could have shrimp for the big game.

November 15

We watched a movie this morning before my family and I went on a driving tour of D.C. We stopped at the Lincoln Memorial and walked over to the Vietnam Veterans Memorial to see Mom's cousin's name etched on the wall. Mom cried. We had a nice ride and got back just in time for the Clemson-Maryland game—they ended up tying.

Mom, Dad, Sandy, and Joe left tonight. It was hard to say goodbye.

November 16

Matt had a good day—he got up several times. In fact, we were on our way to the hospital chapel this morning and we ran into half the Clemson cheerleaders. They visited for about thirty minutes.

Matt and I took a good nap later and afterwards put up our "Do Not Disturb" sign.

I'm here by myself now. With You, Lord. I love You. Thanks for taking care of me!

November 17

Judy and Larry left today. Matt had a good day— he only threw up once! And he got up and walked around several times. Thank You, Lord, for good days!

November 18

I loaded up the car this morning and moved in with Jenné. She and Holly and Mimi are really neat gals, and a definite plus for me during this time. I need the friendship.

I followed Holly over to the apartment and moved my stuff in. I stayed and talked for a while, then went back to the hospital until about 9:00. Jenné and I talked until 12:30. Good night's sleep.

November 19

Matt had a fairly good day. He had a good workout at physical therapy, then started feeling nauseous. He took a nap after lunch and then we got to go outside and walk. It was really cold, so we didn't stay out long.

And so the days drifted by without any kind of routine, except a chemo schedule and our favorite television programs. Yet it was in the everyday aspect of things that we were able to touch each other most deeply. A growing intimacy was spurred on in our just being together—eating together, talking together, getting to know the hospital staff together, learning together, walking together.

Together. That was the beauty of our marriage. Together in the Lord. He was our center. And from Him flowed an overwhelming love for us, through us, for each other. Because of that love, I often found myself getting praise I did not feel worthy of....

November 23

I truly have the most wonderful wife in the world. She puts up with all of my ignorance and loves me in spite of it all. Tonight she left me the sweetest little card for no reason, other than love.

Father, I definitely don't deserve her, but I praise You for bringing her my way. My life is so much richer because of her. Sometimes I wonder what all this would be like without her here, but then I wouldn't want to experience this without her. Lisa is such an encouragement. She helps me through each day.

What am I like since being diagnosed as having cancer? I feel a little different. In fact, I'm bald now and about thirty pounds lighter. I hope to gain the weight back over the next few weeks, I hope in the right places! This doesn't bother me a whole lot, though.

I seem to be having a little problem writing now, for my fingers have become numb and it's harder to control my hand. This is a little aggravating.

I think I'm coming to know more about the Lord through all of this. I find myself saying things that sometimes surprise me. I want to become a more spiritual person that I may be fully utilized of the Lord, for that is what I really want most. I want to fight against the flesh for the spiritual side of things.

I love You, Lord!
Matt

Isn't that what the Christian life is all about? Coming to know the Lord better? Not trying to be anything, just loving Him more and knowing Him better and allowing Him to do the work within us. "For it is God who works in you to will and to act according to His good purpose" (Philippians 2:13).

Norman Douty writes, "If I am to be like Him, then God in His grace must do it, and the sooner I come to recognize it the sooner I will be delivered from another form of bondage. Throw down every endeavor and say, I cannot do it, the more I try the farther I get from His likeness. What shall I do? Ah, the Holy Spirit says, you cannot do it; just withdraw; come out of it. You have been in the arena, you have been endeavoring, you are a failure; come out and sit down, and as you sit there behold Him, look at Him. Don't try to be like Him, just look at Him. Just be occupied with Him. Forget about trying to be like Him. Instead of letting that fill your mind and heart, let Him fill it."

As Matt lay in his hospital bed with little energy for much else, he was open to beholding the Lord, to being occupied with Him. But for Matt, as for everyone, a willful choice was essential. We must make a conscious choice, to look at Him, to seek Him first. And that is not always easy.

I feel so lazy...Matt wrote in his journal one day. Maybe that has been because I haven't done anything in...I don't know how long. I'm beginning to think my brain is becoming inactive, and I'm probably right. I need to find something to do; I just don't know what.

Lord, help me to know what to do with my time. I still want to do something for You. I don't want to become a deadbeat. Help me, Father! Show me which way I should go.

Matt and I both had a tendency to get lazy, to watch too much television, to become complacent, to lie around and let the days slip through our fingers. After all, he was getting better. He may have looked a lot sicker, and he was certainly weaker and much thinner. But we knew that it was just a matter of time before he would complete the treatments and we could get on with our lives.

Thanksgiving was a memorable holiday. The previous year I had spent Thanksgiving Day with Matt and his family, a host of kinfolk, and a table spread with the most wonderful traditional Thanksgiving feast. Celebrating the holidays with lots of food and lots of relatives was not uncommon for the Locke family.

This year would be different, though. Matt and I were disappointed that we couldn't get away to join the family in South Carolina. But we were determined to make our quiet little Thanksgiving together the best possible substitute.

The Atchleys had invited us to "apartment-sit" their condo in McLean, Virginia, so we gratefully left the hospital for a welcome change in our surroundings. A few close friends came over for lunch, my first try at cooking a Thanksgiving Day feast of my own. At least nothing burned!

On Friday, Matt started feeling sick again, so we decided to head back to the hospital a bit earlier than planned. Little did we know what awaited us there.

November 28

The day after Thanksgiving, and we have plenty to be thankful for. We received a pass yesterday and were able to be out for the entire day. It was great being out on pass. Lisa made a Thanksgiving Day feast that was great. We had turkey, dressing, mashed potatoes, gravy, and sweet potato casserole to top it all off. Randy and Susan were able to come up and be with us—it was a wonderful surprise. The rest of the day I wasted watching television programs that were not really important to life.

Now it's Friday, and things are going pretty good. I had a time with getting sick earlier, but that seems to be past for now. I was getting sick so much today that I decided to come back to the hospital earlier. I'm glad I did, because I ran into Uncle Pat, Aunt Claudette, my sister Lisa, Mama, and Daddy coming out of the elevator. It had to be the Lord's intervention that we ran into each other. We had a happy little reunion and a great time together. I slept most of the day, but by evening I was ready to go and we went out for seafood, which was terrific.

Now I'm back at the hospital in my little bed. I think I'm going to have to get one like it when I get back home. I'll need a bed just like this one.

Getting back home is something that I would love to do right now. I just wish I knew when it would be possible. We have to be able to go down for Christmas, we just have to. Lord, please work it out.

I feel much better, Father. Thank You for my health. Thanks for the glory You have been able to receive out of this. Make me more of a man, a Christian man, and one able to really stand up for You.

In addition to all the physical struggles, Matt was struggling with many other decisions. His father kept Matt's name on the payroll at the company, and we accepted those checks as gifts from God and Matt's family. Our church also continued to pay Matt as youth minister, and the church's love and support for us were overwhelming. Yet it was difficult for Matt to have other people taking care of us financially, something he felt he ought to be doing himself, and he struggled with what to do about his position there. Around Christmas, he finally resolved it within himself and wrote the church a letter.

Dear Church Family,

Lisa and I miss you all terribly and would rather be there with you than anywhere else, if only possible. You all are truly family that we wish we were spending this holiday season with, but the Lord has different plans for us this season. Even as I write to you, I'm sitting listening to Christmas music and anticipating its fast approach. If you start to feel sad for us, don't. Lisa and I have been blessed with so much since our marriage. We have each other, we already know the Lord whose birthday we celebrate soon, and our joy will rise with the joy that each of you experience on Christmas Day. I pray that Christmas will make you look at the Gift which God gave to you on Christmas Day long ago, and may your joy be ever more glorious.

I also write to ask that you, as a church body, do something for me that I ask after much thought and prayer. Please accept my resignation as Youth Minister of Pope Drive. I know that you are keeping me on and continuing to send my check out of love, but it is time for someone else to fill the position that I am unable to, nor do I know when I will be able. So please accept my resignation effective immediately. Please do not try to talk me out of this, for I have thought it out long and hard. Know this, too—just because I've resigned doesn't mean that Lisa and I will not be involved deeply when we get back. As I said at the beginning of my letter, all of you are our family now, and we intend to remain as a strong part of this family.

We hope to be home in the next few months. We can't wait to worship with you again. I expect a chance to run my mouth some when we come home, so Brother Kelly beware!

Love forever, in Christ,
Matt

Matt never sent the letter. He couldn't. The church said they wouldn't allow him to resign, and that was that. We were confused and grateful. But it was clear that we had all decided to wait and see what God was going to do.

The doctors said Matt's condition was improving. They said he could be treated as an outpatient after Christmas and recommended that we find an apartment nearby.

With the help of some friends, I was able to find a cozy one-bedroom condominium just a few blocks from the hospital. The furniture we rented didn't half fill the spacious rooms, but we had all we needed. Nothing in the area was cheap, but this place was the most practical and the most reasonable. We needed to be close to the hospital. And with the money we had saved, Matt's checks, and the per diem he would receive as an NIH outpatient, we would have more than enough. Out of the Lord's love and care for us and in response to the prayers of His people, our needs were being met.

With so many people praying, we were certain that good things were going to happen and we waited expectantly to see the mighty power of God. The anticipation was building excitedly as Christmas approached. I had a feeling we would receive some priceless gifts this year.

The news that came a few weeks before Christmas brought excitement and cause for celebration, not that the incarnation of Christ needed any additional joy. But our celebration of the angels' Good News was heightened by the angelic doctors' good news: "You can go home for Christmas. You will be discharged when you return to Bethesda from the holidays. You will be an outpatient. And you know what else? It looks like...we think you're in remission. All the tests and scans show looks like scar tissue."

Could it really be true? Was Matt really healed of this dreaded disease, this cancer? Were his treatments from here on out going to be merely consolidation and recovery? Oh, please be true! Thank You, God, for our miracle! This time the tears in our eyes were from happiness.

Despite the good news, I tried to guard my excitement. Just as I had found it difficult to believe my young husband was dying, I now found it difficult to believe that the very thing that had caused him to be dying was dead itself. Not that I didn't believe in a God of miracles; I sincerely believed that God would heal Matt. But somehow, amidst the belief and faith inside my heart, a gnawing seed of fear and doubt had been planted. And no matter how hard I tried, I couldn't seem to pluck it out before it took root. Was my humanness fighting against my faith? Or was it some sort of premonition? I didn't know. But I was determined to trust and obey the Lord in spite of my feelings.

The week before Christmas, one of Matt's college roommates drove up to visit us one afternoon at our apartment. When Gary and Matt were together they always acted silly, like little boys. They made fun out of the most simple things, and their laughter was contagious.

We all enjoyed a pleasant afternoon together, and as Gary got ready to leave, I made him a little bag of munchies for his trip back. We hugged and said our goodbyes, and Matt walked Gary out to his car. Fifteen minutes later, he still hadn't left. And their uproarious laughter outside our window made me curious. They had taken some crackers from Gary's bag and were throwing bits and pieces to a lively little bushy-tailed squirrel. As it scurried to catch the cracker crumbs they tossed to it, Matt and Gary were completely amused at its antics. What a wholesome and simple form of entertainment for those two handsome young men—and for me. It seemed that every day brought new lessons in how to enjoy and savor the simple things in life.

Matt certainly loved to enjoy life. Often he acted silly to lighten up the mood, or just to tease me. He was at his best when he was making others laugh. One afternoon it was too cold to go outside, but Matt was feeling particularly good and wasn't about to waste an unusual surge of energy. He cranked up some Leon Patillo music on the stereo and started dancing, running around the tables and chairs, jumping up and down, making silly faces. I couldn't keep up with him because I was laughing so hard.

Matt had to keep his plastic "pan" handy in case a sudden wave of nausea came over him. Often he would jerk it up to his face as if he were about to get sick, then turn to me and laugh. "Fooled ya!"

At the hospital, his pranks were becoming notorious. Once a nurse trainee was administering a blood transfusion. She was extremely conscientious; she was also excessively nervous and wanted to do everything just right. When she walked back into the room several minutes after she had started the blood transfusion, Matt began shaking violently. Hurriedly, she began to check over the equipment. "What's wrong? What's wrong?" she asked in a state of near-panic.

And then Matt began to laugh.

"Oh, Matt, don't do that to me!" was her relieved response.

Even the doctors weren't immune to Matt's practical jokes. One morning during routine rounds, a group of doctors and nurses gathered outside his door to discuss Matt's case before examining him. When they entered, Matt had on a pair of "Groucho Marx" glasses, complete with bushy eyebrows, fake nose, and moustache. "You didn't tell me about this side effect to chemotherapy," he teased. Their laughter brightened his day as much as he brightened theirs.

Matt and I found we could enjoy the simplest things in life, especially surprise packages. One arrived from my parents, a huge box that aroused our curiosity. We could hardly wait to drag the box down the hall to our apartment and find out what was inside. We speculated the whole way. Other people may not have been as excited as we were, but Matt and I were delighted when we tore off the wrappings and uncovered ninety-six rolls of brightly colored toilet paper! From that point on, we had one less item on our shopping list.

My journal keeping was sporadic, but on a few occasions I tried to do a little catching up. Some of my recollections weren't pleasant. Looking back now, I am shocked at the selfishness and immaturity that was evident in my attitudes, and probably my actions, as well. My Christmas entry captured a little of my emotions.

Matt's second cycle went much more smoothly than his first. It seemed like he was sick every day of his first cycle. During the second cycle he was out on pass a good bit—we went motel-hopping! (The hospital is no place for honeymooning.)

Day one of cycle three was the day before Christmas Eve. Matt spent the night at the hospital and continued to get hydrated and received anti-emetics.

We walked to the Metro stop to ride to National Airport at 5:30 in the morning. There was a huge crowd at the airport—holiday traffic—and we had to wait in line almost right up until our flight took off. It was delayed about forty-five minutes, and we didn't know if we'd make our Charlotte connection—but then everything was running behind!

We finally made it to Greenville/Spartanburg Airport about thirty minutes late, but there was still a crowd with signs—and a television camera! We knew Bill would be there with his home video camera, but we didn't expect Channel 4 News. I made Matt walk out first, and in his excitement he left me behind....Most of the people there were Matt's family and friends. I remember feeling like I was so far away from home.

It was a lonely ride back to the house, even though we were in a van full of people. Judy and Matt's sister Lisa said something about not wanting me to be left out—they loved me, too. And I cried because I guess I did feel left out.

I almost got over these feelings when we got back to "the old house." It was the first time I had really seen it fixed up. It was empty when I walked through it months ago.

Barbara and Chris had decorated everything so Christmassy. It was beautiful! Yet—it wasn't home. It was like walking into someone else's house, not our own. We had a good visit—we didn't spend much time at the old house. We were at Grandma's and Claudette's and Larry and Judy's. It was good to see everyone, but I missed my own family. It felt strange not being with them on Christmas.

We left early the day after Christmas, and we had another long wait at the airport. We didn't get back to NIH until about six, and they started immediately on Matt's chemo. He left that night—discharged! And we went home to our apartment.

That is all I wrote about our 1986 Christmas, but there was much more. That first night we watched some news segments telling about Matt's progress and hopeful remission. I'll never forget the light in Matt's eyes when he told the reporter, "It's great to just be able to be home—to just be able to be *here*." I knew he was talking about life, not just a place.

Being home was a breath of fresh, life-giving air for Matt. The country fields, the ponds, the trees, the people and place of Honea Path, South Carolina—this was his home. Though being home was special, especially for Christmas, being *here* was a gift, a gift of life that Matt did not take for granted.

Not knowing when we'd be back in South Carolina, we wanted to make the most of that trip home. We received visits from several close friends and did a little visiting ourselves, but most of our time was spent with Matt's family.

Though our things filled the rooms and covered the walls of the old house, it still didn't seem like home. While we had been in Maryland, some United States marshals had issued papers advising us to move from our home as soon as possible. It seemed that another railroad was going to be built, and the track's path was to be twenty-five yards from the front door of our little honeymoon cottage. We didn't know what we were going to do, especially since our attentions were focused on Matt's treatment at the time. But God knew our needs, and He was preparing the way even while we were at NIH.

The Lockes owned a house down the road from their own home, a small country place that had been in the family for years. Matt's great-grandfather had lived in it. They called it "the old house." It was quaint and cozy, its white paint sparkling in the sunshine, the yard shaded by beautiful oak trees. It seems the renter had just moved out, so it was available for us to move in.

While Matt and I were adjusting to our new routine up in Maryland and preoccupied with Matt's illness, his relatives had moved our belongings into the old house. I wasn't sure it was necessary, and I really adored our first little home there. Matt and his family had done so much work on it before we got married, and we hoped to be back there soon. Why go through all the trouble?

But we knew that the move was best for us, allowing us to be near Matt's family and relieving us of any government entanglements because of the proposed railroad. Besides, they had really gone to a lot of trouble to get us moved into the old house, and we arrived to the fresh smell of spiced tea, holiday tunes floating through the air, two beautiful Christmas trees, ribbons and bows, and a fire in the fireplace.

The old house had a certain charm about it. Matt had grown up there—from a three-year-old playing around the barns, climbing the trees, and digging holes in the yard to a teenager worrying about his first date. It was a special place. And though it would be a while before I could think of it as "home," I was warmed and excited by the Christmas atmosphere when we arrived.

The trip home was short, but it was rich in fellowship and love. It energized Matt and gave him a hope and fervor he hadn't felt in months.

We returned to Maryland rested and refreshed. Matt went straight to the hospital for another treatment of chemotherapy, and when he finished we went to our apartment. For the first time since we moved to Maryland, Matt would no longer have to get a pass to leave the hospital. We would both be living in the apartment, a wonderful blessing for this still-newlywed couple. We slept well that night.

With Matt's new status as an outpatient, we got to know a whole new staff. Matt's treatments were in the clinic now, rather than the hospital. And he had been assigned a new doctor. Dr. Stevenson had moved to Bethesda Naval Hospital across the street, and Dr. Junghans became Matt's primary doctor.

Dr. Junghans was tall and thin, more easygoing than Dr. Stevenson. He always had a ready smile and frequently stopped to chat with us. Our doctor-patient relationship quickly grew into a close friendship as well.

Kathy was Matt's new nurse at the clinic. Energetic and joyful, Kathy brought an unending supply of smiles and hope to her patients. We were thankful for these changes. With change comes learning and growing. We were moving on in this saga.

The new year was fast approaching. And for the first time, getting to the end of Matt's treatment was a visible, attainable goal.

Matt received a fresh supply of blood on New Year's Eve. It helped him start off 1987 with an extra boost of energy. To help us ring in the new year, his best friend from home and my college roommate had driven up to Maryland.

Mark had known Matt longer than most people. Through the "daredevil club," motorcycle wrecks, Fellowship of Christian Athletes meetings, and double-dating, the two of them had literally grown up together. When they were in elementary school, they had tried to build a tunnel from Matt's backyard to Mark's. When they were in their early teens, they decided together to be serious about serving the Lord. They had been accountable to each other ever since, and both of them set their hearts on God's will.

Susan had been a dear friend ever since I met her at Clemson. She was always making brownies and other surprises for people and sharing her musical talents—forever pouring herself out to those around her. This was her second visit to Maryland, and she and Mark brought plenty of happiness with which we would start the year.

Randy was another close friend who lived a few hours away in Paradise, Pennsylvania. He called and invited all of us to come up for New Year's Day dinner with his family and Trace, another friend of ours. Not thinking Matt was ready for such a long drive, I was surprised when he said, "Sure, let's go!"

We set out for the Amish country the next morning, and the trip was a wonderful diversion. The drive through the countryside was beautiful, and the company was even more enjoyable.

Randy's family was friendly and down-to-earth, and their warmth made everyone feel welcome in their home. His mother really knew how to cook. She prepared a delectable meal of sauerkraut and sausage, and lots of other New Year traditional dishes. She even made shoo-fly pie for dessert.

We also visited an authentic Amish family to see how they survive using old-world ways in such a modern, technological society.

Late that afternoon we headed back to Maryland. Not long after we left Paradise, the sleet had turned to big flakes of snow. The road was soon blanketed in white, and the skies were dark and foreboding. The heavy snow seemed to be coming at me like flashes of light as I drove slowly onward. The snowflakes were beginning to mesmerize me, and I remember feeling anxious and a little afraid. I had to keep telling myself, *Keep going. Keep driving. It's going to be okay. Just keep going.*

The other three were dozing, and I felt like I was in my own little silent world as snowflakes fell all around me. *I trust You, God. I trust You.*

It seemed as though God was calling me to trust Him for more than just our safe passage back to Bethesda. He was asking me to trust Him with Matt's life as well as my own. He was beckoning me to surrender myself to Him with total abandon. *Yes, I trust You, dear God.*

It took us several extra hours to arrive safely back in Bethesda, and I was exhausted. The next morning, a blanket of stark white snow covered the ground, erasing the ugliness of the muddy roads of the night before. The sky was bright, the air fresh and crisp. I thought of the Lord's cleansing power in our lives. All the dirt and ugliness of sin is cleansed by the purity of the blood of Christ, through His life, His death, and His resurrection. I was sure that this new year would be the same, blotting out all the pain and sorrow of the previous months.

In order to keep track of Matt's progress through the treatments, I had posted some charts on the wall in our living room. Each chemo treatment, each spinal tap, each radiation therapy was marked off on the chart. It was exciting to cross off each one and know it would never have to be dealt with again. We were making it through this ordeal. And if everything went according to schedule, we would be settled back in Honea Path by May, just in time for the wedding of one of Matt's college roommates.

Although our spirits soared as the treatments were marked off our chart one by one, there were a few setbacks along the way. Matt's body was tired of the chemotherapy. The drugs had all but destroyed his bone marrow, so his body was not able to reproduce healthy blood cells very quickly. As a result, his immune system was weakened and he was extremely susceptible to infections, especially at certain times in his treatment cycles. On several occasions, Matt was readmitted to the hospital to be treated for infection.

January 9

Mama and Daddy Locke are here tonight—Matt is still in the hospital. Was it only yesterday he went back in? Please get well and hurry back, my love!

January 13

How the days are swiftly passing...Matt still has fevers. Lord, heal his body of the infection that invades him. Strengthen him and bless his body with Your touch. I wish he could touch the hem of Your garment, Jesus. I love You! Thank you for what You're going to do in our lives.

It wasn't easy, but I was learning how to trust Him with everything. What was He going to do? How did He fit into all this? How did He work into the daily routine of our lives? A more important question: How did we fit into all this? How did we work into His perfect, divine plan? My mind was full of questions.

January 17

> *Lord, what is really happening? Sometimes—no, all the time—I have yet to understand what You are doing with us. Are You preparing us for something greater? I hope so. To serve You in our everyday lives is the highest call.*
>
> *To humble us, to break us is necessary. Keep doing it. We must be totally emptied of "self" before we can really serve You wholeheartedly. I love You!*

Can God only work in our lives to the extent that we choose to let Him? He can certainly thwart our plans at any time He chooses. Often we persist in pursuing our own plans, our own will, thinking that if God truly works all things together for the good of those who love Him, everything will work out okay even if we mess things up ourselves. But wouldn't it be a wiser choice to have a humble and willing spirit, submissive to our wise and holy God? His love and wisdom merit simple, childlike trust in Him. So the question is not "Can we trust Him?" but rather "Will we trust Him?"

It snowed several more times through the winter, and we enjoyed it as much as Matt was able to. One day as the snow floated down onto the already white earth, Matt and I decided to walk down the road and buy some waterproof boots for me. As we walked across the parking lot, we approached some bushes. Suddenly, I found out that despite Matt's illness, he still had plenty of strength in him. He gave me a hardy shove into the big, prickly bushes. This meant war! I struggled to get up while trying to swing him around into the bushes with me. No mercy. He was still stronger than I was, and he kept pushing me down in the snow. We laughed until the tears froze on our faces. Snow-covered and giggling like a couple of children—what a sight we must have been to anyone who might have seen us.

The snow brought many things with it: beauty, freshness, laughter, fun, and new challenges in driving. I drove with extreme caution on the roads, but the tricky part was just getting the car out of the parking lot. Big mounds of snow often blocked the way.

One night Dr. Stevenson called just to check on Matt. We had just come back from supper with Jenné and it was getting rather late. Matt had eaten too much and was getting sick when the phone rang. I talked to Dr. Stevenson for a minute, then Matt came to the phone. By the time he hung up, I was changed and ready for bed.

"You might want to get dressed again," Matt said. "I told Dr. Stevenson we had to shovel our car out of the snow before we could go to the hospital tomorrow, and he wouldn't hear of it. He said he had a few things to take care of, then he was coming over to shovel the car out for us."

Thankful and delighted, we were amazed at this doctor's commitment to his patient's well-being. Yet he was no longer Matt's official doctor. He was doing it out of his love and concern for a friend.

Matt and I were trying to plan a short trip to visit my family in Alabama. The second weekend in February looked free on the calendar. It was shortly after my birthday, and Matt had a break in his treatment schedule. So we bought our plane tickets and made our plans.

Several days before we were supposed to leave, however, Matt started running a fever. Back to the hospital we went. We hoped the infection would be cleared up by Wednesday so we could still leave on Thursday. Was that a risky and ridiculous hope? Matt said he wanted me to fly home to be with my family, even if he couldn't go. But there was no way I was going to leave my husband in Maryland. I didn't want to be apart from him for even a few days. Something would work out.

I had contracted a fairly bad cold and had to wear a hospital mask when I was with Matt. One day, I really wasn't feeling well at all and thought I might just stay in the apartment and rest. But when I spoke with Matt on the phone, he practically begged me to come to the hospital. How could I refuse?

When I got there late that afternoon, Matt was bright-eyed. He was getting aggravated with all "this staying in the hospital stuff," he said, and had decided to go ahead and go to Alabama if he was feeling okay. Then one of the nurses interrupted us and asked me to walk down the hall with her. I followed her into the nurses lounge.

"Surprise! Happy Birthday!"

Balloons, a chocolate cake, a stuffed teddy bear, and a group of smiling nurses greeted me. The tears in my eyes blurred my vision. How thoughtful they were! But this was not anything unusual for this group of special people who did all they could to encourage the patients and their families, who tried to make life as normal as possible.

Matt's birthday gift to me was something I treasured above all of the other flowers and cards and gifts put together. One of the nurses had given him a sheet of computer paper and some magic markers. He made me the most beautiful card I had ever received.

Dearest Love,

I wish I had a fancy card and an expensive present for your birthday, but instead I give you messy handwriting and paper with holes all in it. I wish there was more, much more, that I could give, but there seems to be nothing left to give.

My heart you were given long ago, and you filled it with love overflowing. I gave my heart to you, and I never want it back.

You are the sunshine of my life, and my happiest day was when you became my wife. Can you believe it's been six months? The time seems so short. I wish we had been together for a lifetime and had another one to go.

I'm having a hard time writing to you, because no mere words can express what you mean to me. So I'll stop where I am by saying I LOVE YOU!

What did I ever do to deserve such a deep, rich love from such a wonderful man? How precious and good are the gifts of our Lord.

The next day Matt gave me another beautiful card and a heart-shaped sachet filled with sweet-smelling potpourri. He had given one of the nurses some money and sent her out to buy me something from him for Valentine's Day. Though he was disappointed about not being able to do it himself, he was pleased with the card she selected. She told us it seemed to express what she saw in us. On the front of the white card were big letters, "For My Wife," and underneath that were the words "Your love is a special blessing" positioned above a delicate pink flower. The verse on the inside was beautifully simple: "As we share our love, our faith, and the special joy of marriage, I realize how truly blessed I am to have you for my wife. Happy Valentine's Day." Matt added a sentence of his own: "Thanks for such a great married life. You are the best wife in the world. Love, Matt."

What a special love had grown through this trial. I knew I wasn't the "best wife in the world," but I was to him. And he did not feel like the best husband in the world, but he was to me. "Such a great married life"? Yes. It wasn't the circumstances or possessions or place that determined our joy and love. The Lord had brought us together and was continually working to fulfill His purpose for us and through us. He had poured out His love to us and given us an overflowing love for each other. He made the difference in our marriage.

As much as we loved each other and communicated that love, we continued to hold something back from each other, something that haunted us both in the back of our minds. We never expressed our fears about the possibility of Matt dying.

We clung to every hope we had of his healing, just as we clung to each other. Wanting to be strong and hopeful for each other, neither one of us ever brought up the subject, although we both thought about it.

Against the wishes of some of the doctors, Matt and I made the trip to Alabama. He continued to run a low-grade fever, and his white blood count was rising, so the doctor gave him some antibiotics to take with us.

We felt the time away from the hospital, from Bethesda, would be good for us. And we were looking forward to spending a few days with my family. So we flew out that Thursday morning.

The antibiotics caused Matt to be nauseated, a feeling he was getting quite used to, so we spent much of our time just resting and cuddling in front of the fireplace. We always enjoyed cuddling and fireplaces.

On Friday, some friends came by for a visit. Scott and Matt had been roommates at Clemson, and their friendship was knit tightly together. Scott and his wife Linda had asked Matt to be their baby's godfather, and when Matt had been in the hospital before we moved to Maryland, they had sneaked six-month-old Heather Lynn into Matt's room so he could see his godbaby.

My parents did everything they could to make us comfortable while we were there. And other than Matt's nauseous feeling, our visit was warm and relaxing.

The pastor of their church had asked if either Matt or I would be willing to share a testimony in the Sunday worship service. Matt wasn't feeling up to it, which made me nervous because I knew God wanted me to share what He was doing in our lives. I'd never felt very confident standing up in front of a lot of people, even though the church wasn't very large.

I can't do that, God, I thought. *Matt's the one You want to do that. I don't know what to say. What if I cry? What if I get up there and I can't say anything at all? What if....*

What if you trust Me, my child? What if you rest in My arms and look to Me? What if you take your mind off of what you think and just have faith in Me? I Am...all that you need.

As we expected, Matt wasn't able to go to church for morning worship, so I told the pastor I would like to talk for a few minutes. The moment I walked into the sanctuary, I began to weep. I sensed God's peace, but I could not stop crying. Maybe it was being away from Matt, even for just a few hours. Maybe they were tears that had been held back for a long time and were now bursting forth in release. I wanted to be held. *Oh, God, hold me close to You.*

The pastor called me forward. After drying my tears and regaining my composure, I walked quietly to the front of the church. Standing before the small congregation, I leaned on the podium and told my story. As I talked about Matt's willingness to die, I began to cry again. I barely made it through the next few sentences. I don't remember everything I said, but I noticed that half the church was crying with me.

What a comfort to share tears with friends. They were bearing our burden with us. They were praying for us and loving us like so many of our Christian brothers and sisters were doing across the country. Matt and I were surrounded by so many people who showed God's love and concern, just like the Scripture says: "Carry each other's burdens, and in this way you will fulfill the law of Christ" (Galatians 6:2).

Matt was feeling better in the evening and reluctantly consented to go to church and tell his story. Not that he didn't want to go—in his heart he knew he should; but this would be his first time since the diagnosis to stand in front of a church and talk about his illness and the consequential changes in his life. We walked to the platform together. A chair was set up at the front for him, because he was still very weak and couldn't stand for very long. He sat in the folding chair, and I sat behind him on a bench. I wanted him to know he had my support and love in all things.

Though he was nervous, Matt spoke beautifully, right from his heart. The weakened body, the bald head, the frail voice, the quivering lips—none of them were significant as Matt's inner man showed forth boldly. His heart was the Lord's, and he would bring glory to the Lord in whatever way the Lord chose.

Those people of Forest Hills Baptist Church had been praying earnestly for Matt and me. Our presence there was like answered prayer in their sight. As Matt shared his heart, the people listened intently. They were quietly reverent, radiating love and understanding as Matt and I walked arm-in-arm down the aisle, back to our seats.

"I feel like I'm getting married again," Matt joked aloud.

The stillness was broken as the crowd laughed with us.

We went back to my parents' home and prepared for our return flight to Bethesda early Monday morning.

A few weeks after our trip to Alabama, Matt had a long break in his treatments. We still had a wild spontaneity in our young spirits, so when I suggested that we surprise everyone and drive down to South Carolina, Matt was thrilled. It was probably not a sensible thing to do, but he was ready to be back home again. He was at a good point in his treatment cycle. And he wanted to go.

The drive was about nine hours long, and we headed out early Sunday morning. Matt slept while I drove, and by the time we reached Charlotte, North Carolina, I was feeling pretty sleepy myself. Matt, rested and always adventurous, volunteered to drive the rest of the way.

I tried to rest, but I was too anxious about Matt's driving. He hadn't driven since Christmas, and even then it was on the country roads of Honea Path. But he got us safely home, and we went to the Lockes' house first.

Judy and Lisa were the only ones home, and our presence at the front door provoked gasps of unbelief.

"What are y'all *doing* here? I can't believe you're here! I've been trying to call you all day, and I was sure something was wrong!" A mother's typical response of concern.

We decided to go to our church in the evening, so after a short, enjoyable visit with the family, we got dressed up and headed for the church. We hadn't been to Pope Drive Baptist Church since October, and Matt looked quite different after these months of intensive treatment. If he was anxious about what people might think, he never expressed it. He did mention that he thought Pastor Kelly might ask him to share a testimony. To avoid Matt's having to get up in front of the church, we decided to slip in a little late.

Pope Drive is a large church, and Matt didn't feel confident about speaking in front of everyone at this point. But the Lord had given him something to share, and God's voice was speaking to Matt as we sat through the first part of the service. When Pastor Kelly noticed us sitting in a pew at the back of the church, he asked Matt to come to the front and share from his heart. He did.

After the service, we were greeted with hugs, a few joking comments, and lots of surprised expressions. "We didn't know who that was back there. We thought you were a POW or something until we saw Lisa." We enjoyed the warmth and their surprise at our presence.

The week in South Carolina was a busy one. Though Matt should have been resting, he wanted to do as much as possible while we were home. There were too many people to see and too many things to do.

We spent one day at Clemson talking with special friends. Everybody seemed surprised at how "healthy" Matt looked, considering what he was going through.

But he pushed himself much too hard those first few days. We spent the rest of the week lounging around and resting in front of the warm stove at Matt's parents' house.

When we headed back to Maryland, Matt was running a low-grade fever. He had a problem with mouth sores and not much of an appetite, but his will and determination were strong. As he had said from the start, he was going to fight this thing with everything he had...until the Lord told him to stop fighting.

Matt had nearly completed five cycles of treatment—only three more to go. He had been in and out of the hospital for short-term stays, treatment for infections whenever a fever cropped up. Yet the doctors continued to be optimistic. He was still in remission, and he was nearing the completion of his therapy.

Ben Locke was a little anxious about his first flying trip, and the weather conditions didn't ease his fears. But his older sister Lisa reassured him, and Matt's younger siblings made their solo venture to Bethesda just fine. After a mix-up about where to meet at the airport, Matt and I finally connected with Ben and Lisa, and we all anticipated a good weekend together.

Saturday morning cartoons provided ample entertainment for us before we headed east to Annapolis. Matt's cousin Steve was a midshipman at the Naval Academy, so we decided the four of us would pay him a visit. Steve was a "shave head"—because he was going into the marines after graduation in a few months, the guys in his company had shaved his head the week before, all in keeping with tradition.

Matt's hair had slightly begun to grow back, and the fuzz cropping up gave him the "shave head" look. As we walked around the campus, he seemed to fit right in with those midshipmen. He put in a lot of walking that day.

Not one to complain of feeling weak or tired, Matt often tried to keep going as if everything were normal. He wanted to do everything for himself—and with everyone else—that he was able to do. I didn't want to limit him, so I didn't discourage our walks and visits. One day, though, I realized that a lot of his going and giving was for me.

As Matt and I stood in our living room preparing to go on yet another outing, he looked at me with sad eyes.

"I think you forget sometimes that I'm not as strong or as healthy as I used to be," he said with a tired voice. "You can't expect me to be able to do all I used to do."

My eyes didn't cry, but my heart did. Maybe I did expect too much from him. I never forgot about his condition; it was constantly staring me in the face. I just wanted him to live as close to "normal" as possible and to be able to do everything he wanted to do. It was important to let him know I had confidence in him, in his abilities. I didn't want him to think that I didn't believe in him, that he couldn't do whatever he set his mind to.

It was almost a tug of war. I stood on one side of the rope saying, *I'll encourage you to do whatever you can because I know you can do it, and I know you really want to even though you probably shouldn't.*

Matt, on the other side, pulled in frustration: *I'll do all I can because you want me to and you think I can, even though I don't really feel like it.*

What a jumble of thoughts and feelings! Love, concern, fear, ambiguity, pride, frustration—they were all present in these struggles with the will. "What do you really want from me?!"

More adjustments to this growing relationship and strengthening trial. The balance came in our honesty with God and each other. To first please Him, to first love Him, to first seek His face, and then to love each other, to please each other, and to put each other's wants before our own. Communication was the all-important factor. We couldn't "do" or "be" without knowing.

"Dear friends, let us love one another, for love comes from God. Everyone who loves has been born of God and knows God. Whoever does not love does not know God, because God is love" (1 John 4:7-8).

In early March, my mother and my younger sister Becky came to visit us for a week. One day Matt wasn't feeling like getting out, or maybe he just wanted some time alone for a bit of reflection. So he backed out of our sight-seeing excursion to Washington, D.C., and told me to go on with my mom and sister. He would be all right by himself for a while.

After we left, Matt pulled our little love seat around to face the window. There he sat with his tape recorder, his thoughts, his God. He recorded what he was feeling that day, some deep things that he had been struggling with for a long time.

"...and, uh," Matt had begun to speak before the tape was recording. "I guess I haven't been too used to speaking lately. I just wanted to try to put down a few thoughts of what I've been going through lately—things that have been on my mind, things that maybe I've kept quiet about. And I just wanted to let loose and say whatever comes to my mind right now. I wanted to say a little bit about me, I guess. And I figure here in the quiet of the room is one of the best times, while I'm alone with just You and me, Lord, where I could get a few things out in the open.

"First of all, Father, I just want to say 'forgive me.' Forgive me for not being what I know I can be for You. These past months have been some rough times, nothing worse than what some of the early Christians went through. I may have suffered some, but I haven't suffered for You. I feel so lax, so lax because of my slackness and my times to talk with You and my daily Bible readings—they'd become so routine, and now I've gotten away from it. Maybe that's good, in a way, because I see that's what it had become—a routine for me. And it wasn't really alive.

"If there's one thing I don't want to be it's a boring Christian, 'cause there's too much excitement in being a Christian.

"Lord, I want to thank You for giving me a second chance—a second chance at life, 'cause when you approach the closeness of death, you begin to look at things in a different light. You begin to look at yourself and wonder if you had gone on, what kind of mark would you have made on the world? What would people remember you for?

"Would you be remembered as some nice kid, some nice kid who was always polite to the adults, loved kids, loved to talk? What good is that? What real impact have you made on somebody's life? Be remembered for those things? No, what I really want to be remembered for is what I've done for You. That's all that really matters anyway. So why don't I do more?

"Maybe it's because I didn't really want to in the past, not really deep down. I said I did. But I wasn't willing to give up so many things. So many things were blocking my time with You, so many things that were just taking me away from opportunities to do things for You.

"Oh, but thanks for the times alone, Lord, like now. Thanks for giving me a chance to understand myself, because that's something I often don't do. I don't understand myself.

For so much of my life I've gone through it with sort of a fakeness, I guess.

"I was a good kid. Never got into much trouble. Well, really, I never got into any trouble. I was always thought of being a 'holy' person. But You know different, Lord. You know the real me, and You always have. And that's scary sometimes, because I don't want anybody to know the real me. 'Cause the real me is a different person; it's what's inside. It's the thoughts going on when I'm doing something which I may say is for You, but it's really for me, something that's being done for my gain and not Yours. It may look good on the outside, and people may praise me for it. But You know better, and You know my selfish reasons.

"Lord, thanks for always being there. Thanks for always caring. Thanks for all You've given. Thanks for this time to be able to share with You, and just let things out..."

Matt struggled, as we all do, with his humanity, his old nature. Yet he saw himself in a way totally different from the way others saw him. Matt Locke was this together, down-to-earth, humble, friendly, charming young man who walked closely with the Lord. His heart's desire was to live the abundant life Jesus calls us to. But he struggled with acting on this desire, with his new nature overruling his old nature, like Paul wrote about in Romans 7.

"So I find this law at work: When I want to do good, evil is right there with me. For in my inner being I delight in God's law; but I see another law at work in the members of my body, waging war against the law of my mind and making me a prisoner of the law of sin at work within my members" (Romans 7:21-23).

If our body is constantly waging war against itself, how can we possibly win?

"This is the victory that has overcome the world, even our faith. Who is it that overcomes the world? Only he who believes that Jesus is the Son of God" (1 John 5:4).

"His divine power has given us everything we need for life and godliness through our knowledge of Him who called us by His own glory and goodness. Through these He has given us His very great and precious promises so that through them we may participate in the divine nature and escape corruption in the world caused by evil desires" (2 Peter 1:3-4).

Jesus provides all we need, and our faith in the truth of that brings victory.

Our Anderson church family was getting excited about our return. When we saw our friends at Pope Drive in February, they were eagerly asking when we would be coming home. A youth rally was scheduled for March 21 and Matt was asked to speak if he thought he might feel up to it. The rally fell during a slow time in Matt's treatment cycle, and Matt was not one to turn down an opportunity to talk about the Lord. So we marked it on our calendar and made plane reservations to South Carolina.

The week before the youth rally, Matt seemed a bit more restless than usual. He was thinking a lot about the rally, speaking at church in front of lots of people, not feeling very confident. He spent hours thinking, writing, and praying about what he would say.

We flew to South Carolina on Friday, and all Matt could think about was Saturday night. He spent several hours by himself the next morning, walking in the woods, resting out on the pond in the little boat, relaxing, thinking, talking with Jesus. What was the Lord telling him?

He let me read the testimony he had written out a few days before. It was all about what was happening to him physically—finding out about the cancer, the time in the hospital in Anderson, his treatments at Bethesda. He closed with "I've been in Maryland ever since that day, and things have been going wonderful. They believe the cancer has disappeared, and I'm on my way to being normal again." *Normal again?* I thought to myself. *Will things ever be normal again? What is "normal"? Is anything normal in this life?*

That evening Matt seemed extremely nervous. I could certainly understand why. He was weak and tired. And he was a little self-conscious about the way he looked—bald, skinny, frail, pale. But Matt radiated something from within that distracted people from his physical appearance. I continually prayed for God's peace to fill him.

The service was widely publicized in the area, and the church was packed with people of all ages. My parents and younger sister and one of her friends drove up for the weekend to be with us. We sat together toward the front of the auditorium. A group named "Eternity" would sing for the first part of the service, and then Matt would speak. When he was finished, the band would close with a few more songs.

"Eternity" was bright and polished, good-looking and beautiful. Their spirit matched their appearance. We enjoyed their music, although Matt still looked a little apprehensive. But the Lord had given him a message to share, and what he said that night was far from the testimony he had let me read earlier. Instead, a deeper message of the inner man came out boldly.

We had been sitting on the second row with our backs to the crowded auditorium, so when Matt got up on the platform, he was startled by the size of his audience. A quiet hush fell over the place.

"Great day!" he exclaimed as his eyes scanned the room.

"I was a little nervous about all this...uh...before I got up...now I'm a little nervous about this after I've gotten up. But the music and everything has really helped to put me at ease a lot.

"Uh...I guess the best place to start with all this would be at the beginning. Everything...I'd just graduated from Clemson University in May. And, uh, things were going real good. I hadn't gotten a million-dollar-a-year job, or anything, that I was looking for. But, uh, everything was going fine. And I'd just gotten married in August—that's a date I guess I better not forget. And I was working two jobs. I'd just accepted the job at Pope Drive, too, and I was working for my dad. And everything was going great, and I felt like I was on top of the world. And I thought everything was going for me, you know, everything was going good. Then all of a sudden I get this news that something's wrong.

"It started out, I started having pains in my abdomen and my back. At first I tried to ignore it because I didn't have insurance. And, uh, I put up with it for a while, and tried to put it off until I did have insurance—which may have been a stupid thing. And after a while I couldn't anymore because it was too painful.

"So I finally went to the doctor, and the doctor began to run a series of tests. And after several tests, they called me in and my wife and my mama and my daddy and my aunt. And when all these people are sitting in a doctor's office, you start to wonder if maybe something's wrong.

"So we're all sitting in there, and the doctor tells me, 'There's a chance you may have what we call "lymphoma," which is a type of cancer.'

"Cancer. That's all I need, I thought. I mean, I've been healthy all my life." His voice began to quiver a bit, and his eyes welled up with tears.

"And, uh, I'd been into weight-lifting, and I thought I was pretty bad," he joked to lighten the mood. "I could put my brothers and my daddy down, anyway.

"But my world sort of seemed to be crashing in around me all of a sudden. I'd, uh, I'd always been bad about brushing things off, so of course I didn't cry. And I just tried to smile through it knowing that, well, maybe something's going to happen for the best out of this.

"Well, we went on and commenced to having other tests. And they scheduled me for surgery. And I believe it was on the nineteenth of October. It was a Sunday. And they scheduled me for surgery, and they went in and found out it was lymphoma, a special kind called 'Burkitt's lymphoma.' And they told me after I came out that I may have six weeks to live.

"Well, I've always been able to accept whatever the Lord threw at me, I guess. There was a verse that I thought of then. It says, 'According to my earnest expectation and hope that I shall not be put to shame in anything, but that with all boldness, Christ even now as always will be exalted in my body, whether by life or by death. For to me to live is Christ, and to die is gain.'

"And that was hard for me to believe, a little easier to say. But I really did believe that then. But I'm glad that the Lord saw fit to give me another chance. I've had a special opportunity a lot of people haven't. It's a little different after you've gone through it one time, and tasted of near death, and then you look back over your life again. And the big thing that you do is say, 'If I had gone on, what would my life have accounted for? What did I do for the Lord's glory?' Because you begin to see that's the only thing that matters.

"You see, we get so caught up in this world sometimes, so caught up in the things the world shows us on the TV set, the wonderful things that they show—new cars, new homes. None of it amounts to a hill of beans. It's all what you do for the Lord. And so often we never see that until it's too late.

"Like I said, I was given another chance. I was able to see it. And I want my life to count today, to count today for eternity.

"There's so many people that are watching you. So many people that are watching to see if it really works for you. And what are we showing them? So often I think we don't show what the Lord would really have us do.

"Are our lives the living examples they should be for the Lord, for Christ? Have we really turned it all over to Him, or are we still holding things back?

"I learned some little things in my own life that I was still holding back while I was in the hospital. I got to be a TV addict. I'd sit and watch TV for hours—there was nothing else for me to do, 'cause I was laid up in a hospital bed...at least I thought. Then I got to thinking one night when I was laid up in the hospital, and my wife was there with me, as she always was. I got to thinking about, you know, I could really be using my time more constructively. I could really be making a difference for the Lord even here—through prayer, through reading His Word.

"But we always say we don't have time, because we use our time on other things. Maybe it's time we woke and looked at the world around us and what's going on. Don't let the Lord have to bring you to a point where you have to stare death in the face before you really look up to Him. Use the chance you have right now. Use the chance He's given you right now for Him, the life you have.

"Reach out to those people around you that you've always thought about reaching out to. Visit that person in the hospital that you've always thought about visiting. We waste so much time doing little piddly things, and not enough time doing things for the kingdom. Well, let's start doing things for the kingdom. And let's really learn what it's like to be a Christian. I don't think many of us know. Let's really learn what it's like to follow Jesus Christ, holding nothing back—even your own life, if you have to.

"If the Lord could have gotten more glory from my life taking me on when He...when He could have, I wish He had. I love this world, but I can't wait to be with my Savior some day. And if there are any of you here tonight who don't know Jesus as your Lord and Savior, I pray you'll make that decision tonight before you leave this place.

"You're not promised tomorrow. He doesn't promise any of us. I don't care who you are. I don't care how popular you are. I don't care how much money you have. I don't care how much status you have in the community. The Lord's not promising you tomorrow.

"But He's given you today, and He's given you right now. And He's given you a decision, too. And He leaves it all up to us...to decide whether to serve Him or whether not.

"Thanks for just giving me the opportunity to stand before you and share a little bit about me, a little bit about what the Lord's done in my life. I just pray His love will really enrich your life, too. Thank you."

As Matt poured out his heart, the only sounds in the auditorium were occasional sniffles and a little bit of laughter. His voice was feeble, but his message couldn't have been more powerful.

Matt was a startling contrast to the highly polished, attractive singing group. Yet he spoke with boldness and brilliance. He was a humbled and broken vessel wanting only to please his Creator. His message was from God.

After the service, he was immediately surrounded. People were encouraging Matt and showing their love and compassion for him. The drummer from "Eternity" came over to me.

"I want you to know I'm praying for you," he said, "because I know that whatever you're going through, you two are going through it together."

My eyes clouded with tears. So many times I had felt left out as people showed their love and concern for Matt. I was thankful for this sensitive, understanding man who showed compassion for us both. We *were* going through it together. We were sharing the emotional pain and heartache. I only wished I could have shared some of Matt's physical pain as well, especially later that night.

We didn't get to bed until midnight. Not long after we settled into bed, Matt began to toss and turn. Then he began to grimace and grunt in pain. Cringing and turning, he held on to his right hip. He cried out as the pain increased.

Oh, how helpless I felt! I wanted so very badly to do something—anything—but I didn't know what I could do. The phone wasn't even hooked up yet at the old house.

"Let's go back to your parents' house and call the doctors at NIH," I suggested.

We got dressed and Matt hobbled out to the car. It hurt me so badly to see his face contorted with pain. He was frustrated, too. Nothing he did seemed to ease the pain. Until he sat down in the car. I breathed a quick prayer of thanks.

Our parents were laughing and talking at the kitchen table, and we took them completely by surprise when we burst through the back door. Amidst his grunts of pain, Matt explained the problem while I called the doctor. Judy headed for the bathroom to see what she could find. Matt's doctor was not on call, so we talked to his nurse, Sandy. She said she would talk to the doctor on duty and call us right back.

I continually prayed that Matt would have some relief from this awful pain. I had never seen him like this before, and I knew it had to be unbearable for him to let it show. He always tried to keep his suffering hidden so the rest of us wouldn't worry. Now, even sitting down didn't help him any. I wanted so badly to take his pain and suffering and put it in my own body, just to give him some relief.

Judy found some painkillers in the medicine cabinet, and the doctor at the hospital said it was okay for Matt to take them until we returned to Maryland and they could see him at the hospital.

The pain subsided a bit under the influence of the painkillers, and we were able to get a little rest that night when we finally got back to our house. Matt was supposed to teach a combined youth Sunday school class the next morning, but he didn't think he could do it. So I agreed to fill in.

We were so tired, and Matt was still hurting when we got up. He didn't know if he would be able to sit through Sunday school and the morning worship service, too. We brought along an extra supply of painkillers just in case.

I hadn't prepared a lesson for Sunday school, so I decided to tell three different love stories. I had read a lot about Jeremiah the past few days and I wanted to share what I had learned about this prophet's love and commitment to God. Though rejected and despised by many, the "weeping prophet" held on to God and continued to fulfill God's calling in his life.

Some of my favorite passages were from this book, and they offered assurance for Matt and me during this struggle we were going through. "'For I know the plans I have for you,' declares the Lord, 'plans to prosper you and not to harm you, plans to give you hope and a future. Then you will call upon me and come and pray to me, and I will listen to you. You will seek me and find me when you seek me with all your heart'" (Jeremiah 29:11-13).

We were seeking Him. We would find Him. We had to trust in Him to fulfill His plans. He already knew them, but we had to be patient, waiting on Him to show us how to follow Him.

The second love story was a bit more personal. The group was delighted and attentive as I shared with them our own love story.

When Matt and I first met, I recognized something different about him. *We could be great friends*, I thought to myself. As our friendship grew, both of us began to feel a desire for something more, something deeper, in our relationship. I didn't tell Matt how I felt, and I didn't know exactly how he felt about me.

One afternoon, I happened to see Matt with a girl he had been dating. They were with another couple, and the four of them were planning to go on a singles retreat together for the weekend. My heart sank. Matt had such charm; of course other girls would enjoy his company. But he had led me to believe that there was something special about our relationship. I had thought that he was attracted to me, but now I wondered if it was all in my head.

Shortly after the two couples left for the retreat, I went into a room by myself to talk to God. I poured out my heart to Him, and I let go of my own will, desiring only His.

Okay, God. I'm going to stop planning, stop wishing for what I want. I will rejoice in You and be satisfied with You. I love You, Lord.

Peace flooded my soul as I spent those hours in fellowship with God. During the weekend, I participated in a fast for World Hunger at the Baptist Student Union at Clemson. My mind, body, and spirit were refreshed and renewed.

Tuesday night was the first time I saw Matt after the weekend retreat. During a BSU council meeting, I looked over at him and was overwhelmed with gratitude for what God had given me in this special friend. I had to tell him. Quietly, I wrote him a little note. *Matt, I'm so glad you're my friend. Love, Lisa.*

His face lit up as he read the note, and he began scribbling a note back to me. *Lisa, I'm glad you're my friend, too. What are you doing Saturday night?*

Thus began our romance....

Then I told about another part of our love story, about a year and a half after the note incident. May 1, 1985, was the day before spring semester exams during our junior year. While I was getting ready to go to my job at a balloon gift shop, Matt called. I told him I was on my way out the door, but he said if I would wait for him to get there, he would give me a ride to the shop. A ride would be much quicker than the ten-minute walk, and of course I loved spending every chance I could with Matt. So I waited.

Soon he was at my door with a rose in hand and his eyes shining brightly.

"Oh!" I exclaimed. "How beautiful! What's it for?"

"Read the card," Matt responded with a grin.

He gently handed me the rose. I took a deep breath of its sweet fragrance before pulling out the little card. *Dearest Lisa, Just as this rose symbolizes life and love, I want to spend my life loving you. Will you marry me? Love, Matt.*

I didn't know what to do, so I screamed. "Are you serious?!" The love in his eyes said it all. "Yes!" I answered emphatically.

He told me to put the rose in some water. As I unwrapped the green florist paper from its thorny stem, something shiny caught my eye. A beautiful marquis diamond ring was resting on the rose's stem. More surprised than ever, I slipped the ring off the flower and put it on my finger. It was official. We were engaged to be married.

As I shared our story, there were "oohs" and "aahs" from the girls in the room, and the guys asked Matt for some pointers in being romantic.

The final story I told completed the lesson, and appropriately so, for it is the most complete love story of all—God's love for us. This love that is immeasurable, this love that surpasses knowledge, this love that is higher than the heavens, this love that died for us and was resurrected for us, this love that lives forever. Oh, how I wanted to convey the message of His love for us. Nothing else was quite as important. And when we see His love for us, it constrains us to obey Him, to have the attitude of Paul—and of Matt: "For to me to live is Christ, to die is gain."

As I repeated those words from Philippians 1:21 in that Sunday school class, tears began to stream down my face. Several others in the room shared those tears with me. And I prayed, knowing my tears were touching God's heart.

When we got back to NIH, the doctor checked Matt and prescribed a stronger pain medication. This leg and hip pain was persistent, probably a pulled muscle. Nothing relieved it for long. Matt's mother had bought him a cane, and he used it often.

Matt had always been so healthy, so physically fit, and it frustrated him to not be able to get around as much as he wanted to. Still, we got out as much as he could.

We had watched the brightly colored leaves of autumn fade into the snow-covered months of winter and then melt into a vibrant array of new life. As the temperature climbed higher, the D.C. area exploded in color. Never before had I seen such a brilliant display.

Matt and I took advantage of the warm sunny days and went for walks several times a week. We found paths alongside streams and through wooded areas not far from our apartment. It was wonderful just to be outside, to walk along in God's beautiful creation, to talk intimately together. Matt loved the outdoors, and he longed more than ever to be home, to be in his own fields, beside his own streams and in his own woods. When were we finally going to get back to South Carolina?

We took countless drives through the outskirts of the city, down the Potomac. Splurging on a pair of binoculars, we learned to enjoy watching both birds and people. Often we sat quietly by the river, listening to the sounds of the water rushing over the rocks, the birds singing sweet songs to each other, the people talking and laughing. We relished the beauty of everything we saw.

Because Matt loved the country so much, I often searched for a new rural route on our sightseeing excursions. Many times we stopped the car to get out and walk. On several occasions we visited Great Falls Park, along the Potomac River. Away from the noise and the exhaust-clouded air of the busy city, away from the antiseptic smells and sterile halls of NIH, out here where the birds sang and the wind rustled through the trees and the water splashed against the rocks, we had found a sanctuary.

We spent countless hours at Great Falls, sometimes talking breathlessly as we walked, sometimes walking in silence. Words weren't always necessary.

One Saturday morning, we settled into the car and decided to head in a different direction. Matt's nurse Sandy was from Frederick, Maryland, and she often spoke of the serenity and scenic beauty of the mountainous region where she lived. A historic little town with preserved buildings and tailored neighborhoods, Frederick sounded like paradise.

On the way out the door, I grabbed a bag of stale bread. "Let's take this along in case we see a duck pond or something," I joked.

The scenic forty-five minute drive to Frederick was relaxing and enjoyable. As we turned down one of the main roads, I noticed a "Historic District" sign.

"Why don't we check that out?" I suggested. Matt agreed.

Winding around the corner, we drove through an immaculate residential area. Just ahead we could see what looked like a small park. As we got closer, we were delighted to see that in the middle of the park was a large, sparkling duck pond!

Matt had really been missing home, and one thing he had especially missed was the two-acre pond on his parents' land. Matt would spend hours down at the pond swimming, feeding the ducks, rowing in the little boat, or just enjoying the spectacular view.

We decided to park the car, walk around the pond, and use up the stale bread we had brought along. Eight or nine ducks waddled our way when we started tossing out bits of bread from our perch on some rocks. One of the birds was either extremely hungry or exceptionally greedy. As Matt threw pieces of bread, this duck would chase away the other ducks and gobble up the bread. It was eating most of the crumbs we tossed out!

Matt began to laugh at the greedy duck. He laughed loudly, happily. I laughed, too, more at Matt's laughter than at the duck. How precious that laughter was! Again I learned how to delight in the small treasures of this life which are rich in value. I thought again of Paul's words of wisdom, "Command those who are rich in this present world not to be arrogant nor to put their hope in wealth, which is so uncertain, but to put their hope in God, who richly provides us with everything for our enjoyment" (1 Timothy 6:17).

God used so many people to brighten our time in Maryland. Matt's family, my family, numerous friends from South Carolina who drove up, flew up, called, wrote letters. We were so loved. There was so much *life* around us, so much life inside us wanting to be lived. And though weakened physically, Matt was determined not to let his physical limitations keep him from missing out on life.

Some days Matt missed out without even realizing it. After one of his treatments at the clinic, Matt was still groggy and light-headed from his medication. But he was hungry, and after thinking for a few minutes, he decided he was hungry for hot dogs and tater tots. We didn't have either at the apartment, so I told him I would drop him off at home and stop by the store down the road. No, he said, he felt fine; he would go to the store with me.

After boiling the hot dogs and baking the tater tots, we sat down in front of our feast. The tater tots weren't very crispy, but we ate them anyway. A few days later, I asked Matt what he would like for lunch. We had some hot dogs and tater tots left, I told him, and he said that would be fine. This time I fried the tater tots.

As we ate, I commented on how much better these fried tater tots were than the baked ones we had eaten earlier.

"When did we have these before?" Matt asked with a puzzled expression on his face.

"The other day, after your treatment. Don't you remember? You were hungry for hot dogs and tater tots, so we went to the store to get some and then ate them for dinner."

"Are you kidding? I must have been so drugged up I didn't know what was going on. I don't remember any of that!" Matt's medication to combat the nausea was obviously affecting his mind as well.

One weekend my older sister Sandy came to visit. Matt loved laughing at Saturday morning cartoons, so he encouraged us to go out together without him. Don't worry, he said, he'd make "good use" of his time alone. We left him watching cartoons, and Sandy and I took a subway ride to D.C. As we walked out to the mall, we noticed several colorful kites dotting the skies. We walked over by the Washington Monument and saw even more kites. There were hundreds of them, every design and shape and color imaginable! Their bright colors drifted lazily across the sky above us.

When we walked further around the monument, we saw a crowd of kite makers proudly showing off their original designs. We had stumbled upon a kite contest! One by one, they presented their crafts in front of the judges, proudly displaying their works of art.

How romantic the kites seemed! Brightly soaring high above us, lofty and proud, the kites towered over the watching crowd. What would it be like to fly like that? To soar above the world? Yet those kites were on a string, controlled by the flyer. Sometimes the wind caught one and it drifted away on its own little path. But most often, the kite was sent up and brought back down at the will of the one who held on to the string. Sometimes the kite would drift toward the trees and power lines; knowing the kite would be damaged, the flyer jerked it away and "led" it in a different direction.

Some days I felt just like one of those kites. My life was controlled by my Designer, and I often felt as if I was soaring above the world, flying proud and high, lofty, bright. Sometimes I felt the wind trying to carry me away. And then I felt as though I was being jerked away from the direction of my own "flight plan." Yet wasn't it always and only for my own good? To continue in the direction I wanted to go was not always good for me; indeed, it could sometimes be damaging to my purpose in life, God's purpose for me.

"And we know that in all things God works for the good of those who love Him, those who are called according to His purpose" (Romans 8:28). I knew that He knew best, and I was determined to follow His leading in my life.

Matt's parents came to visit us the weekend before Easter. A friend of mine from high school was also visiting, and on Saturday morning the five of us took the subway into D.C. We didn't realize that the entire city would be out. It was Cherry Blossom Festival time. What a crowd! What a mistake! We fought the crowds all day long, and it was miserable for Matt. Still, we had a good time just being together. We saw magnificent tulips—some of them three feet tall—and flowers of every color blooming all over the city. We stopped to sit on the grass and watched a rugby game for a while. We watched people walking past, some leisurely, some hurriedly. Where was everybody going? Where were we going? Why did we have to be going anywhere at all? Was just "being" enough for this life?

I'd been asking myself a lot of the same questions. What was the point of all this? What was the purpose of life? I knew that "God works for the good of those who love Him, who are called according to His purpose. For those God foreknew He also predestined to be conformed to the likeness of His Son...that the life of Jesus may also be revealed in our body.... Therefore we do not lose heart. Though outwardly we are wasting away, yet inwardly we are being renewed day by day. For our light and momentary troubles are achieving for us an eternal glory that far outweighs them all. So we fix our eyes on what is unseen. For what is seen is temporary, but what is unseen is eternal" (Romans 8:28-29; 2 Corinthians 2:10, 16-18).

Reality lies in the unseen, eternal things, not these physical earth-bound "jars of clay." We were learning to set our hearts and minds on things above, not earthly things. For we died, and our life was now hidden with Christ in God. Love and security held us in His hands.

Although every day should be a celebration of Christ's life and resurrection, the following Sunday was a special day set aside just for that—Easter. Matt and I awoke early to attend a sunrise service. We wanted to go to one over in D.C., but we weren't exactly sure how to get there.

"Let's just start driving, and we'll find it," I suggested.

So we got in the car and headed for Washington. On the way we saw several cars headed in the same direction. Thinking they might be going to the sunrise service, we followed them as they wove through town. We ended up at Arlington Cemetery. It wasn't exactly the service we were looking for, but since they were holding one, too, we decided to stay.

The skies were overcast and drizzly, but the service was beautiful. It was conducted entirely by military personnel, and their words made the gospel message powerfully clear. The chaplain of the U.S. Army led us in a few songs of worship and then told the triumphant story of Christ's resurrection.

How could anyone sit through this service and not realize the truth of Jesus? I wondered silently. My heart was filled with thankfulness and wonder at the love and sacrifice of Christ. He counted us worth dying for. Did I have such love and devotion to Him?

When Matt and I returned to our apartment, we went back to bed and slept until the afternoon. Later, I gave him a surprise—a small basket filled with his favorite sweets and a cross-stitched picture I had been working on for months. It was a scene with two Precious Moments angels, a little boy and a little girl, sitting atop a silver-lined cloud. Underneath them were the words, "Love goes on forever." Not only would God's perfect love last eternally, our love rooted in Christ would also go on forever.

The following week I began to realize how quickly time was passing. We had crossed off all but one of Matt's treatment cycles on our wall poster. We couldn't wait to cross it off, as well. Then we would be going home! Our excitement was building daily. Once again, I tried to catch up in my journal.

April 9

I knew this would happen—the days of our stay in Bethesda are coming to a close, and I haven't written about our time here as faithfully and as detailed as I would like to have done. More than capturing the events and day-to-day routine, I would like to have recorded the feelings and struggles—the spiritual and emotional battles, the way God has drawn us to Him and to each other. He has created such a strong emotional bond between Matt and me. We know we can always count on each other to be there.

I have to dig deep down inside for this stuff because the words and thoughts are not coming easily. They aren't flowing as they do when I feel like I have to write, as if a dam is bursting inside.

Lord, guide each decision that we make. Teach us not to just "float" along, but to be directed by Your voice, Your Word, Your hand. Thank You for Your gentle leading.

Also around that time, the pastor of my parents' church in Alabama asked us to write a short testimony for their newsletter. Always bad about procrastinating, I put something together at the last minute and had it in the mail just in time.

While I was preparing dinner one night, I could hear Matt yelling for me as he showered. Thinking he might have fallen or hurt himself in some way, I dashed to the bathroom to help him. As I burst through the door, he peered out from behind the shower curtain with a shower cap on his bald head and a sneaky grin on his face.

"Are you all right?" I asked breathlessly.

"Yeah, but I didn't get my hair wet, did I?" he laughed.

Most of you know that cancer treatments have left Matt with a bald head. But that was one of the lighter moments since he began treatment for lymphoma last October.

The past six months have brought tears of sadness and joy, and extended kindness and comfort of family and friends. But most of all, we have experienced the total provisions and limitless love of our God.

It has been an amazing journey into a deeper faith and dependence on our Lord Jesus. We realized we are nothing without Him, especially on that day we were told Matt had six weeks to live if he didn't receive treatment soon.

He was facing death, and I was facing the fact that I might lose the man I wanted to spend my life with. A fresh impression of a truth I had known was made in my heart that day: We are not in control of our lives. But by yielding to God's control and committing our every day to Him, we can experience peace and joy. I can't express in words the calm assurance that fills my heart when I say, "I trust You with my life, Lord, and with Matt's life. You are sovereign." It's not always easy to say, "Not my will, but Thine," especially when Matt is in pain. But it is always the best thing to do.

Through the cycles of his last treatment, Matt has suffered so much, and I have wanted to be strong for him. He has been weakened by the chemotherapy and its side effects. He has had one pain after another in several different parts of his body. And sometimes it seems like the hurting will never go away. On those days, I get frustrated and feel helpless because I can't do anything to ease the pain for him.

To watch my husband go through so many painful experiences, or rather, to go through them with him, has at times left me emotionally, mentally, and spiritually exhausted. It is only through trusting Christ and relying on the promises of His Word that we are able to be lifted above our circumstances. What a comfort to know that we are in the care of our Savior!

So many truths such as that one have been re-emphasized to us through these months. God loves us—what a profound and wonderful thing! He continues to care for us in every way.

Also, in our case, He continues to use His people to minister to us. Matt and I have been blessed and encouraged by the prayers, cards, and letters, and other "love offerings" of Christians. You have helped us through this time.

Matt will have completed all eight cycles of chemotherapy by the time you read this letter. We are thankful and excited and looking forward to what the Lord has in store for us. It's frightening to think about a relapse of the cancer in the future, so we don't. We're trusting the Lord to guide us each day, and we're resting in His love and care. That's the best way to spend this time on earth.

I felt confident about what I had written as I sealed it in an envelope and sent it off to Alabama. But something dreadful happened between the time I sent the letter and the time it was to be printed in the newsletter. We were forced to think about that thing that was frightening to us. I would have to edit that last paragraph, and I was scared. Reality had overtaken our hopes of Matt's completion of the treatments and our returning to South Carolina to stay.

The persistent and aggravating pain in Matt's right hip would not quit. Not only did it continue to plague him, it also began to spread down his leg and toward his lower back. The physical therapy he was going through didn't provide much help, and neither did the pain medication. More tests were ordered. His treatments would continue.

Matt seemed to be most comfortable sitting in a car, so we did more driving through the countryside for the next few weeks. On one trip, we listened to a tape of a Sunday evening service from his family's church. His sister sang in an ensemble, and the group had led in worship that night. Halfway through the tape, a familiar song began to play. It was one of Matt's favorites, one he had often sung himself. A sweet, beautiful voice lifted the melody softly. Matt began to cry.

"It's taken a lot for her to be able to sing again," he whispered softly. He knew of his sister's struggles, yet he also knew of her God-given talent. Though he wanted so much for his family to love and serve the Lord as he did, he knew it was a choice each one of them had to make personally. As his sister sang on that tape, Matt's face shone with love and tenderness.

He had a deep love and concern for his family. He missed them dearly, and though they were close in spirit, he felt so very far away from home. In spite of the distance, we were able to keep in close contact with them. His family called faithfully every night to keep abreast of what was going on. It helped and encouraged Matt to talk with them each night. He longed to be home. When would we be there to stay? Our next visit home would not be what we had envisioned.

With his last treatment coming up, we were hoping to return to South Carolina for good. Yet I had a hard time visualizing what might lie ahead for us. It was virtually impossible to imagine Matt and me in our home, having children, growing old together. I longed for those things so much, but my heart grew sad because I would not let myself think about them. Somehow I felt I would have to let go of all my dreams.

The news came as a shock, even more startling than the first time. Matt's doctor called us into his office on Monday. The last cycle of Matt's treatment was scheduled to begin on Thursday.

"We've looked at some of the test results, and we're not exactly sure what we're seeing."

Inside I already knew. The fears I'd tried to push away were forcing themselves into reality.

"There's a small mass in the rectal area, and it may be lymphoma. We're not sure. I've scheduled a biopsy for Wednesday."

Oh, God, please, not more cancer. Cancer—dreaded disease draining life from so many in this world, rapidly invading a body near defenseless against the carcinogenic weapons, gross, ugly, dark sickness. *Please, God, don't let there be more.*

We went back to the apartment with crushed spirits. The dreaded "what ifs" plagued my mind. *What if it is more cancer? What if Matt dies? What if I have to live without him for the rest of my life?*

I found myself wanting to hold on to Matt as tightly as I could. *You gave him to me, God,* I thought. *Why would You want to take this precious gift away from me now?*

We laid down on the couch and held each other close. For hours we caressed and kissed each other as our bodies and our spirits were one. Even as we held tightly to each other, my mind taunted me. *This is the last time we'll ever be able to do this. This is the last time we'll hold each other like this.* I tried to stop the horrible thoughts. *Where is your faith? Where is your hope? Don't be anxious about anything. We are in the Lord's hands.*

The next day, we both just wanted to get away for a while. We went for a long drive down to Skyline Drive, part of the Blue Ridge Parkway in the scenic mountains of Virginia. Slowly and serenely, we drove up the curving, winding roads, stopping several times to take pictures or to get a closer look at the wildlife. What a gracious God we have to create such glorious things for us to enjoy! We reveled in the majestic grandeur of God's handiwork.

On our return trip that afternoon, only the music of Twila Paris broke the silence.

> "Breaking my heart,
> You've been breaking my heart again,
> Making me start again,
> Breaking my heart."

The lyrics of the song really hit me, my heart crying out with Twila's every word.

"That's what I feel like..." I said, keeping my eyes on the road in front of me.

"Yeah, me too."

Often I wondered why God allowed our hearts to be so broken. My thoughts went in circles. *Well, why not us? We're not promised anything in this life. I must trust God no matter what happens. But sometimes it hurts to let go of those things that are most dear to me. Well, maybe if I didn't hold on so tightly to them, it wouldn't be quite as painful when I have to let go. Maybe it's not so much that it will be less painful, but I will have a greater capacity to trust God in all things because of the pain.*

The next day we went in for the biopsy. Three enemas, waiting, pre-medication, then the surgery. Reluctantly, the doctors let me in the room to hold Matt's hand as they performed the biopsy. Though he grimaced and cried in pain, he did not remember it because of the pre-medication. When it was over, we went home and slept.

Me, Matt, and Jenné

Matt was feeling okay when we woke up, so we decided to go ahead with the plans we'd made for the night. Jenné, Mimi, and Holly had invited us over for a cookout at their apartment.

As we walked outside, we noticed the weather had cooled off since that afternoon. It also looked like it might rain.

"I'd better get our jackets," I said. Handing the keys to Matt, I asked him to go ahead and get in the car while I ran back to get the jackets. I didn't want him to have to walk all the way back to the apartment. His energy level was pretty low these days.

As I ran back with our jackets, I was startled when Matt drove up to meet me. He was still a little groggy from the medication that afternoon, and I felt more than a little nervous about him driving.

"Do you want me to drive?" I asked, hoping he would move on over and let me get behind the wheel.

"No, I'll drive."

Okay, I debated, *should I submit to my husband, or should I insist on driving myself?* Jenné didn't live far from us, about three miles. He said he felt fine. He wanted to drive. I would submit.

On the way over there, Matt chuckled as I braced myself. With my seat belt securely in place, I held tightly to the door handle as Matt whipped around the corners and swung wildly around curves. I prayed every inch of the way. When we arrived safely at our destination, I laughed with relief.

We enjoyed the evening with our friends, although Matt fell asleep on their couch early in the evening. We decided to just let him sleep while we talked. He needed the rest. We had a big day ahead of us.

Thursday morning, we went back to the clinic. This treatment would be Matt's final one! We could cross off the last squares on the poster in our living room. We could move back to South Carolina and let Matt recover from the effects of chemotherapy. Everything was going to be okay. Better than okay, everything was going to be great. We could see the light at the end of the tunnel. We could once again dare to dream those beautiful dreams for our life together.

Kathy, Matt's clinic nurse, had brought a celebration feast—ice cream, nuts, toppings—we were going to have a sundae party to celebrate Matt's last treatment.

"Matt, we're going to hold off on your treatment until we find out the results from the biopsy." His doctor didn't look very optimistic. "It just wouldn't make sense to go ahead with the treatment if it isn't doing any good." *If it isn't doing any good? Did that mean there was more cancer?* If it was still in his body, he said, then several of the doctors would have a conference about what to do next.

Our hearts sank. It just didn't seem right. What had the past six months been for? What was God doing? We tried to smile and hope for the best. And we decided to have our little party anyway. We couldn't let all that good ice cream go to waste. Besides, we could have another party when the last treatment really did come.

We tried to sleep that night, but it wasn't easy. I wanted to be as close to Matt as I possibly could, so I snuggled up next to his body throughout the night, nearly pushing him off the bed a few times. I just wanted to hold on to him, to hold him with me as long as I could. I kept trying to push away the awful thoughts that haunted me. *He won't be here with you much longer. You'll be leaving Maryland soon, and you'll be leaving alone. He won't be a part of your future.*

Oh, God! I cried. *I want to trust You—not only with my life, but with Matt's life, too. I'm afraid.*

I tried to remember all the verses I could to drive away the fear. "Cast all your anxiety on Him because He cares for you" (2 Peter 5:7). "For God did not give us a spirit of fear, but one of power, of love, and a sound mind" (2 Timothy 1:7). "For you did not receive a spirit that makes you a slave again to fear, but you received the spirit of sonship. And by Him we cry, 'Abba, Father'" (Romans 8:15).

We slept late the next morning, but neither of us felt very rested. Trembling all over, I felt like I had a lump in my throat and a knot in my stomach. The biopsy results were supposed to be in today.

Matt's nurse called to see if we could come in and talk to his doctor before noon. We went up to the hospital, straight to the clinic, right into the doctor's office. Another doctor was with him. The serious look of concern in their eyes spoke before their words ever did.

We all sat down. I sat close to Matt, holding his hand tightly. My palms were sweaty and my throat was dry. I couldn't begin to imagine what Matt was feeling at that moment.

"We got the biopsy report back," the doctor said. He looked as if he might cry. "Matt, there's more lymphoma."

My reaction was the same as the first time we heard that word. My heart ached, my chin quivered, and my eyes flooded with tears. *Now what do we do?* I thought to myself. Wayward teardrops escaped from my eyes and slid down my face, and then I couldn't hold them back any longer. Matt remained composed and strong, as always, as if he had already known what to expect.

The doctors went on talking about options and treatments. Matt was sensitive to their position. It can't be easy to be the bearer of such devastating news.

"I'm sorry y'all had to be the ones to tell me this. I know it's hard." Even as this darkness was falling upon him, Matt was thinking of others' feelings.

"I suggest you go back home for the weekend. Come back to Maryland on Monday or Tuesday, and we'll let you know what we've decided is best as far as further treatments are concerned."

His doctor was thinking of us, too. Matt needed to be home in South Carolina with the rest of his family. He needed the extra support and encouragement before entering this dark tunnel. Or, dreaded thought, is it a cave? At that moment, it was too dark to tell.

Hastily, we made arrangements to go to South Carolina for the weekend. We went home and packed, then called our families. Matt's parents would pick us up at the airport; mine would come to South Carolina and meet us there.

When we arrived, there was a feeling of tension and anxiety. Matt's family tried to be positive, but the smiles were strained, the laughter forced.

After the initial face-to-face sharing of Matt's latest prognosis, we all wanted to make the weekend count. Encouraged by Judy and Larry, we decided to enjoy our time together no matter what. And we did.

The Lockes: me, Matt, Judy, Russ, Larry, David, and Matt's sister Lisa

We ate too much. We took long walks. We played charades. We laughed. We were hopeful, positive, encouraged, believing in miracles. Suddenly, it seemed like everything was going to be okay. People were still praying for Matt to be healed, and nothing was impossible with God. I genuinely believed that the Lord was allowing everything to get so bleak and dim that we could not help but to trust in Him and believe in Him for a miracle.

The doctor called us later that weekend, interrupting our happy times with the sad reality of Matt's relapse and the need for further treatment. They had decided on the next step, he said. The salvage protocol "BACT," designed for patients who failed their first protocol, was the consensus. He thought Matt would be back on Monday, but we hadn't scheduled our return flight until Tuesday. Matt would start on BACT as soon as we returned on Tuesday.

BACT was an acronym, each letter standing for the name of a drug Matt would receive. We were told that he would be given high dosages of four very toxic chemicals for five consecutive days. If the cancer didn't kill him, the treatment might. It was hardly a positive outlook. Should he risk it? He had to. It was his only hope.

At that point in our lives, it was not easy to hold on to the truths of God's Word. In reality, Matt was victorious through Christ no matter what happened. If the Lord chose to heal him, we would praise God. His healing would be to the glory of God. If he died, he would go to a far greater home, a perfect, eternal heaven with Jesus. For to Matt, to live was Christ and to die was gain. Matt was "more than a conqueror through Him who loved us" (Romans 8:37).

Yet all we could see at the time was that our dreams were in a tailspin, spiraling rapidly downward. Hopeful for his healing, but realistic about the doctors' prognosis, we saw from our limited human perspective. And it was painful.

At the airport on Tuesday morning, our goodbyes were cautious. In the back of our minds we wondered if—no! We couldn't even think that this might be Matt's final goodbye. We would all be together one day. We just didn't know the time or place.

A quiet flight back.

A silent ride to the apartment.

What was Matt thinking about?

"I'm glad everybody had a good time this weekend. It was good to see everyone laughing," he said.

"Yeah, it was a good weekend, wasn't it?"

Early on the afternoon of April 28, Matt began the salvage protocol. Many of the fears and anxieties he had been holding inside came spilling out after he received his pre-medication. As a side effect of the drugs, he was not in complete control of his words or his actions. He said things that didn't even make sense. He laughed nervously. He grasped at things that weren't there. He was acting so silly that I wanted to laugh. I cried instead.

His doctor would do a spinal tap in the clinic, and then we would wheel him up to the hospital unit, a familiar place. He would be readmitted as an inpatient for the duration of these treatments.

The doctor had a difficult time with the spinal tap. Matt kept turning around and talking nonsensically. When the doctor finally finished the procedure, Matt had to lie flat for a while. With his eyes closed he kept puckering his lips as if to kiss someone, and he reached out his arms as if to hug someone. Who was he thinking of? He opened his eyes and looked at me. Flinging his arms around me, he pulled me close to him. I choked back the tears and rested my head on his chest. *Oh, Matt, where are you?*

When it was time for him to go to a room, the nurse and I helped him into a wheelchair. As we wheeled him up to the thirteenth floor, he talked non-stop, never really saying anything. As soon as he was settled in his bed, the treatment began.

Though they had always been open with us, the hospital staff seemed to know something I didn't. Was this all for nought? Was it just one big experiment, the outcome of which they already knew?

Matt had become a special friend of many of the doctors and nurses at NIH. They were distressed about his condition, and they were doing everything they could to help him. Maybe they, too, were hoping against hope that Matt would be all right. Maybe they didn't want to openly admit that there was not much hope, that the outlook was grim. But God was still in control. The hospital staff could only do so much, but they could not go beyond the sovereignty of God.

The five days of Matt's intensive treatment was very stressful, but he would not remember much of it. For his protection, he was sedated heavily. The drugs caused him to release a lot of pent-up emotions. For the first time since he was diagnosed, Matt and I shared our heartaches and tears. Though he never remembered those special times, we cried together often, comforting each other, praying together, weeping together. A few of the nurses even cried with us.

We cried because of the pain—emotional and physical. We cried because of the suffering—it hurt us so very deeply. We cried because of the impending reality—Matt was dying.

Thursday meant Matt only had two more days of treatment left. It also meant that his parents and my mother would be with us. They had made plans to come when they realized the seriousness of the situation. I was staying at the hospital with Matt; they would stay in our apartment.

I was thankful to be with my husband as much as possible, but I was also becoming exhausted for lack of rest. The emotional strain was also deeply stressful, and my body ached nearly as much as my heart. I wanted to care for Matt as best I could, but I didn't want him to think I thought he was totally helpless. He was a strong-willed man who liked to do everything for himself. How humbling this ordeal was for both of us.

Matt often needed help just getting around, and sometimes he couldn't even get out of bed by himself. For someone who had always worked so hard to maintain physical health and strength, it was incredibly humiliating.

"Lisa, don't leave me. Please stay with me. I'm like a small child. I can't even go to the bathroom by myself. This is so hard for me...."

His voice, so soft and sweet, was accompanied by tears, both mine and his.

"It's hard for me, too, honey." I held him close to me. *Oh, God, when will this end?*

Throughout the week, the Word of God gave me something to hold on to. I started reading the book of Philippians, a chapter each night. Each night, different verses spoke to me. It was as if the Lord had opened His mouth to minister directly to me. My heart was strengthened with the joy of the Lord, and my spirit was calmed by His peace.

In the first chapter, I saw what I referred to as "Matt's verses." Verses 20 and 21 had become precious to us. My parents had given me a new Bible a few months earlier with my married name engraved on the cover. It was the New International Version and was slightly different from the wording Matt had quoted in his testimony, but the message spoke loud and clear.

"I eagerly expect and hope that I will in no way be ashamed, but will have sufficient courage so that now as always Christ will be exalted in my body, whether by life or by death. For to me, to live is Christ and to die is gain." Verse 23 continued, "I desire to depart and be with Christ, which is better by far...."

Chapter 2 brought me hope which I held on to faithfully. The exhortation to imitate Christ's humility, His obedience, the glory He will receive in being exalted by God, the name above every name—they were all beautiful to me. Yet, at this time in my life, verse 27 stood out. "Indeed he was ill, and almost died. But God had mercy on him, and not on him only but also on me, to spare me sorrow upon sorrow."

Is this verse for me, Lord? Oh, please let it be my promise. You're going to spare Matt, not only showing mercy on him, but on me also, for You don't want me to suffer sorrow upon sorrow.

There were more treasures to be found in the big little book. In chapter 3, Paul wrote about placing no confidence in the flesh, counting everything loss for Christ, committing oneself to Him in reckless abandonment, pressing on toward the goal: Jesus Christ. Verses 20 and 21 held a blessed reminder, "But our citizenship is in heaven. And we eagerly await a Savior from there, the Lord Jesus Christ, who, by the power that enables Him to bring everything under His control, will transform our lowly bodies so that they will be like His glorious body."

Familiar verses in chapter 4 encouraged me to praise the Lord. "Rejoice in the Lord always. I will say it again: Rejoice! Let your gentleness be evident to all. The Lord is near. Do not be anxious about anything, but in everything, by prayer and petition, with thanksgiving, present your requests to God. And the peace of God, which transcends all understanding, will guard your hearts and minds in Christ Jesus. Finally, brothers, whatever is true, whatever is noble, whatever is right, whatever is pure, whatever is lovely, whatever is admirable—if anything is excellent or praiseworthy—think about such things" (Philippians 4:4-8).

I determined I would do just that. And when my thoughts would start to wander, when my heart would feel sad, I would repeat some of those verses in my mind, sometimes even out loud. *Rejoice in the Lord always. Thank You, God. I count it all joy....*

Saturday was a welcome day. Matt completed his additional therapy, and the doctors even let him leave the hospital. I was sure it meant that Matt was doing okay. But they probably were just allowing him to spend time away from the hospital with me, with his parents, while he was able to—before anything might happen. Even so, we held on to the hope that Matt was going to be healed. His doctor said Matt had responded positively to the additional treatments. Maybe...maybe our miracle was happening!

Matt was deeply emotional the next few days. He cried with his mother; he cried with his father. He allowed his feelings to show freely, though he did not actually talk about them much. On Sunday we took his father to the airport. Before we dropped him off, we took a long ride through the country. The mood was peaceful and hopeful. We were glad to be together.

As we drove up to the airport, Matt's eyes filled with tears. He got out of the car to hug his father and tell him goodbye. As his father walked away, Matt cried silently, not looking back. Was he thinking it might be his last goodbye? Was he thinking about the day when we would never have to say goodbye again?

Over the next week, Matt was able to be out on pass quite a bit. In the mornings, he went in to the hospital for a checkup, then they let him leave again. Of course he didn't feel much like getting out and about, so we stayed in the apartment most of the time. He seemed to be feeling better and our hopes of a miracle were growing.

Because of the subtle improvements in his condition, our mothers felt comfortable about leaving Maryland. Their flights were scheduled for May 9, the day before Mother's Day. Both of them had given so much of themselves, as only a mother could. A few days before, Matt began to run a low-grade fever. Judy was anxious about leaving, but we assured her we would be all right.

On Saturday I drove our mothers to the airport to catch their flights back to South Carolina and Alabama. While I was driving back to the hospital, a lonely feeling came over me. I had a sudden urge to buy a bag of cookies and eat the whole thing. *Why do I want to do this?* I argued with myself. At that point, I wasn't terribly concerned with a healthy diet. I gave in. Driving to a nearby grocery store, I was both embarrassed and determined. Why was I acting this way? Before the day was over, I had eaten every cookie in that entire bag. Suddenly, I felt a little foolish. It would be so easy to start pitying myself. Alone in a big city, my young husband dying of cancer, married less than nine months, most of those spent in the hospital, and now...well, we just didn't know what was ahead.

It's not always easy to keep walking when we can't see where we're going. But isn't that what faith is all about? "Trust in the Lord with all your heart and don't lean on your own understanding. In all your ways acknowledge Him, and He will direct your path" (Proverbs 3:5-6).

By Monday Matt's fever was down, and although he had to stay in the hospital overnight, his doctor said we could take walks in the afternoons. The staff knew how much Matt like the outdoors.

One day after lunch, Matt and I strolled around for a while and ended up at the playground adjacent to the towering clinical center. Like cautious children first experiencing these wonderful toys, we tried out each piece of equipment. We stopped at the swings, slowly rocking back and forth. As we sat there, swinging gently in those little seats, I asked Matt about some of his dreams.

Staring at ground beneath him, he shuffled his feet. "I'm almost afraid to dream any more..." he whispered sadly.

My heart broke. I wanted to hold him close and say, *Let's dream about our eternal home, about kneeling together at the throne of God, about praising Jesus together forever. Let's dream big, happy dreams of miracles and songs and smiling faces.* I wanted to be strong and encouraging. But as I knelt down in front of him and held his hands, looking up into his tear-filled eyes, all I could manage was, "Please hold on to your dreams, because...because that's all we have right now."

Inward struggles. Wanting to be free to dream and hope and live, but bound by reality. We were drifting along, not knowing what each day held. Wrestling with God for what we wanted. Discovering the true joy and peace beyond understanding in submission to Him.

Not planning any specific destination, Matt and I took off one afternoon in a spontaneous drive. We ended up on the George Washington Parkway headed toward Alexandria. The bright, sunshiny day attracted crowds of people to a certain spot on the Potomac—upriver from the airport. Soccer games, wind-surfing, frisbee tossing, laying out in the sun—leisure activities for a lazy weekend. Others just walked along the river or sat and watched the planes flying in and out of the airport.

We walked over to a choice spot by the river's edge. Matt had his brimmed gray hat covering his bald head. He didn't go many places without his hat any more. It was classy looking. He had bought it several years before for my birthday.

As we sat down on the grass, I stretched my legs out and Matt sat in front of me. He leaned back against my chest and tipped his hat over his forehead. With his arms intertwined with mine, we sat in silence watching the planes. It was fascinating to see the frequency with which they landed and took off, one right after another. Engineered by skillful controllers, the airport was operating smoothly and securely. Soon we would be on one of those planes headed home, I hoped.

Relaxed and tired, Matt dozed off in my lap. I leaned back and listened to the sounds of life around us, watching people who didn't seem to have a care in the world. Running, laughing, playing, eating, talking, just having a good time. Did they ever think about Jesus? Did they ever stop and just be thankful for the life and the energy and the blessings they had been given? It didn't seem fair. Matt had so much life in him, so much to live for. I sat there quietly, watching, wondering.

Matt woke up and stroked my arms, yet neither of us said anything. We were lost in our own thoughts, our own little worlds, in the midst of this loud and festive atmosphere. We didn't seem to belong.

Soon we headed back to the apartment—in silence.

We had planned to sneak off to Annapolis, Maryland, to watch some graduation week activities at the naval college. The Blue Angels were going to perform some high-speed maneuvers in an airshow on Monday, and Matt was really looking forward to seeing it.

Monday morning, however, our plans came to an abrupt halt when Matt's temperature began to rise. He was put back on antibiotics to combat the fever, and the doctors decided to keep him at the hospital for observation. He didn't hide his disappointment.

Later that morning, one of the psychiatric nurses asked if Matt would mind being interviewed by some local medical students. They were studying bedside manner and were learning how to be sensitive to the needs of patients.

As the group came into Matt's room, I recognized the doctor accompanying the students. He had been with a group that interviewed us during our first week at NIH, seven months before. I wondered what changes he saw. Did he see the depth of love, the strengthened bond that had developed between Matt and me over that time?

Matt was hot and flushed, so they cut down the time they had allotted for questions. One of the students asked about the adjustment we had made because of Matt's illness, and I remember him saying something about not being the kind of husband he wanted to be.

My throat began to ache as the tears stung my eyes. Matt had been feeling so guilty about his inadequacies. Yet he was more than I ever dreamed I would have in a husband. Just being with him made me feel special. I loved him more than I had ever loved anyone in my life, more than myself.

As we sat on his hospital bed facing those medical students, my mind and heart were full of words I wanted to say, but I choked back sobs instead.

"What is your greatest fear now?" the doctor who accompanied the students asked us.

"If the cancer should ever come back." In those few words, Matt verbalized both his greatest hope and his greatest fear. To fear that the cancer would ever come back was also to hope it was already gone.

Mine remained unspoken. I did not want Matt to know that my greatest fear was his death. Or maybe not so much his death as having to live on without him. I wanted to hold on to him with every ounce of strength I had.

Matt's feeble body was defenseless against the fever-causing infection. His blood count would not remain stable, and it continued to decline. His bone marrow could not produce the much-needed red blood cells very efficiently.

The doctors tried one drug after another to try to combat the infection, but nothing seemed to work. By Wednesday, Matt was drained from the continual fighting. His temperature was consistently high, at times reaching 104 degrees. He could neither rest nor sleep. He had a hard time just lying still. As the fever raged on, he became delirious and incoherent.

I couldn't force myself to leave him, even for a short while. So I stayed at the hospital day and night. Often I would lie down beside him on his bed and hold his head against my chest as I prayed for him. He always thanked me. Kind and gentle Matt. Always loving. Yet he seemed to be in another world, oblivious to the seriousness of his condition. Was this a kind of protective mechanism that God had implanted in the human body? Whatever it was, it made me feel lonely. It seemed that I was more aware of his pain than he was.

Throughout the week, Matt went through numerous tests as the doctors tried to determine the source of his infection so they could treat it more effectively. We were constantly making trips down to the x-ray unit on the ground floor. During one of those trips, I had wheeled him down to wait for yet another x-ray and turned his wheelchair around to face me as we sat in the waiting room.

Though he was extremely weak, he sat so tall and straight, almost stately. His face was so innocent, his mouth barely smiling, his eyes reflecting deep, deep love—and pain. As his gaze caught mine, we stared at each other in the stillness of the moment. How I loved to look into his eyes! Such love and beauty were there. For several minutes we looked at each other, and then I couldn't bear it any more. I looked away. Then a thought struck me. How many more times would I be able to gaze into those beautiful eyes? I quickly raised my head and looked intently at him, trying to get him to return my gaze once again. But his eyes were downcast. We sat there in silence.

Thursday was a restless night for us both. Around midnight, Matt's fever went up to 105 degrees. He was miserable, and I helped several nurses give him an alcohol rubdown to cool his sweltering body. He began to shiver and complain, burning up and shaking with cold at the same time. He was uncomfortable and feeling drained, and I hurt for him.

As the shift was about to change, Matt's nurse was concerned about there not being enough help available. She decided to work the next shift as well, to care for Matt through the night.

Neither of us got much sleep, and it wasn't long before the doctors were gathered outside the door for Friday morning rounds. I overheard Matt's doctor talking, and I strained to listen to what they were saying.

"We have reason to believe that all the cancer is gone," he was saying, "but he's suffering from an acute infection." With that, the door opened and a group of doctors came into the room for a few moments.

Did I hear him right? Was he talking about Matt? My exhaustion faded away as I clung to the hope of those words. Another patient on the same treatment stopped by the room later that morning. P.J. was a few years younger than Matt and several treatments behind him on the protocol schedule. He said he knew Matt wasn't feeling well, but he had heard that Matt's cancer was gone and came by to say congratulations.

My spirits soared. Was it really true? Oh, if Matt could just hold on until his bone marrow recovered, until his body was strengthened, until his blood count started to rise again—he was going to be okay!

"Matt! Did you hear that? They said your cancer is gone! You just have to hold on and make it through this fever!"

His response was weak, but his smile conveyed the wonder and surprise he felt. "That's great."

The news seemed like a fairy tale. I wanted so desperately to believe it, but one look at Matt's broken and weakened body made me skeptical. He still needed constant monitoring, more than they could give him here. It didn't seem possible that he was almost well.

Around lunch time, the doctor came in to talk to us. He said they were considering putting Matt in the intensive care unit so he could receive "continuous and more sophisticated care." I didn't want to think about Matt being hooked up to a bunch of machines in some dark corner of ICU, but I knew it was inevitable. His doctor decided it would be best for Matt to have the constant attention he needed right now.

As they began to prepare Matt for the move to ICU, my exhaustion overwhelmed me, and I wanted to run out of the room and find a quiet place to be alone with my tears. I gave Matt a hug and a kiss and quickly left the room. One of the nurses ran after me, hugged me, and let me cry on her shoulder. I needed that. I always tried to be strong and positive for Matt's sake, but the sadness was just so intense. Out there in the hall, away from Matt, the tears flowed freely.

Matt would be undergoing tests and other procedures as they moved him into ICU, so I could not see him for several hours. I rushed upstairs to see Jenné's roommate, Holly, who was a recreational therapist in the children's cancer unit.

"They're taking Matt to ICU," I told her. Again, the tears began to flow.

She asked if there was anything she could do, and I knew she was serious. Jenné and Mimi were out of town for the weekend, but she was available in any way we needed her.

Our friend Mark was flying in that evening. Could she meet him at the airport? Yes.

I went back to the apartment to rest and clean up. Later, I went back to the hospital to see if I could join Matt yet. Matt's doctor was there, and he said he needed to talk to me. We sat down in the tiny waiting room down the hall from ICU. The atmosphere was dark and stifling. As we sat facing each other on the hard couch, the doctor took a deep breath.

"I guess you know the situation looks pretty grim," he began.

As he explained just what "the situation" was and what "pretty grim" meant, I could feel my heart begin to ache and my throat begin to tighten. As the tears blurred my vision, I couldn't respond with anything but nods. He squeezed my hand and left me alone, and I rushed over to Holly's apartment. Mark was there waiting. Another shoulder to cry on.

"It doesn't look like things are going to turn out the way we had hoped, Mark," I whispered, choking on my tears. Things had never looked this bleak before. The news that the cancer was gone had been such a ray of hope, and now, suddenly, Matt had taken a turn for the worse. The killer cancer was gone. But a deadly fever had invaded that precious, weak body. I had never felt so alone.

Yet Jesus was there. He was loving me through Mark, through Holly, through His presence. He was real to me, and His joy was my strength, the only strength I had.

Calling our families with the news was not easy, but God's grace was sufficient, as it always is. Matt's family would be flying in the next day, and so would my parents. Holly and her boyfriend, Dave, would pick them up at the airport, find them a place to stay, and bring us food. Some of Matt's relatives lived in nearby towns; they, too, would be there to help out. God always provided for our needs, no matter what they were.

The next few days were a blur of feelings, emotions, tears, questions—each minute was precious. I don't think Matt fully understood what was going on, but he seemed to accept it with grace.

There were wires and tubes protruding from his frail body. He was covered with bruises because of a low platelet count. His skin was parched and red. His weakened body shook with a steady twitch. Yet he looked so sweet and innocent. His face would often radiate with an angelic smile. He seemed to be at peace within.

But I could not sense the peace yet. My strong will continued to battle with God. *I'm not letting go, Lord. I still believe You're going to heal him. I'm not giving up, Lord.*

And in my heart, a still, small voice would respond. *I am going to heal him, Lisa. In My way. Trust Me.*

Deep inside, I could sense the pages turning. A chapter of my life was coming to a close. Our time in Maryland was winding down. Our apartment lease ran out in a few days. Everything was pointing toward what I refused to believe.

Unintentionally, Matt provided a lot of humor for us, lightening up the somber, almost mournful mood of our spirits.

He continued to smile, and he was always polite. He even thanked the nurses for drawing blood. His southern drawl could be heard through the ICU area, "Thank you sooooo much!"

Sometimes he decided he was ready to leave the hospital, and he would start to get out of bed. Then came a startling realization, "I don't have any clothes on! Please bring me my clothes, I'm ready to go."

Often he would hallucinate, seeing monkeys and all sorts of interesting things. Once as Mark walked into the room Matt exclaimed, "Mark, you've got bubble gum under your arms!"

As I sat beside him one afternoon, he began to sing a pop song called "Disco Duck." Mark and Matt's brother Ben walked in and chuckled.

"Matt, why are you singing that? Why don't we sing another song? How about this one?" Mark started us on the chorus of "Amazing Grace." Matt sang out loud and clear, with a grace and beauty that touched me deeply. I could only sit there and listen. He was so happy to be singing.

Once, in the crowd of visitors around his bed, he couldn't see me. "Where's my wife?" he asked again and again. "I'm so proud of her!" As they often did that week, my eyes clouded with tears. *If he could only know how proud I am of him, how much I love him. Oh, God, please let him know....*

He talked to people who were not there, or perhaps the rest of us just couldn't see them. Maybe angels were surrounding his bed. I was alone with him when he spoke to a "heavenly messenger" on one occasion.

"Sing? Yes, I sing. I haven't been able to sing real good since I've been sick. But I'll sing again one day when I get all healed up."

What kind of healing was he thinking about? And when would "one day" come? I could see that it was not far off.

The staff in ICU was efficient and gracious. They monitored Matt with quiet expertise, yet they allowed us many privileges in staying by his side at all hours of the day and night. It was a strange and scary atmosphere for the patients, dark and forboding.

As the doctors delivered the harsh but not unexpected notice that they had done all they could do, they decided to move us back to Matt's old room, with his regular nurses and familiar surroundings. We could all be together with him in the spacious room, and there was a window for the sunlight to shine through.

"Isn't it good that we can all be together like this..." I remember him saying.

As he spent the day just lying still and breathing, the room became filled with a sense of love and peace. I know the presence of the Lord was there. Even in our deep sadness, His joy was alive in us. We played beautiful praise music through most of the day, and the room was filled with a quiet holiness.

We had all stayed up with Matt the night before and were exhausted. I kept hoping Jesus would walk into the room and say, "Get up Matt. You're healed." But I knew that I must surrender to His will, not hold on to mine. *Okay, Lord, He is yours. Thank You for sharing him with me. I know I'll be okay...with You.*

Tired, yet peaceful, I laid down beside Matt and fell asleep. When I woke up, I noticed that his breathing had become more labored. His nurses assured us that the way he sounded did not reflect how he felt. A morphine drip in his IV decreased his pain substantially. He kept fighting to breath as I snuggled up to him and sang and talked to him.

"Matt, you're about to be with Jesus. I'm going to miss you so badly. But I'll be okay. You're going home! I'll be there too, one day, and you better be waiting to greet me." Words from the heart mingled with joy and pain. What a paradox of emotions!

"You know he's fighting for you," one of his nurses whispered to me.

"Yes."

Why wasn't it me? Why couldn't I have been the one to suffer so? Everybody loved Matt—he was important to people. Why couldn't I be the one...dying...instead of him?

Knowing it was only Matt's body dying there, realizing the truth of our hope of heaven, I was jealous. Matt was about to move on to a greater life. He was going to be in the very presence of Jesus! His life was not over—it was really just beginning.

And yet I had to linger here on earth. I had to go on without him. I had to experience the pain of separation, of missing him, of ugly memories of his suffering. No, love is not jealous. I loved him too much to be feeling this way. I would not want him to have to face the pain of my earthly death. I became thankful that he was going to leave for his new Home before I did. I was excited for him.

In that crowded hospital room, Matt was surrounded by the people who loved him best, those he loved with all his heart. The doctors say Matt died at 7:15 on the evening of May 27, 1987. But I know that was the day he really started to live.

What strange and wonderful, mysterious and beautiful turns my life has taken since then. Trusting in our sovereign God is not always easy, but obedience and devotion to Jesus Christ is what matters in this life. There is nothing greater on earth than an intimate relationship with the living, perfect God—communion with the Almighty, daily abiding in Christ.

If there is one thing I've learned, it's that this earthly life is temporal and the next life is eternal—so doesn't it make sense to invest ourselves in eternal things *now?* Matt and I were newlyweds—we thought we had a whole life ahead of us. He was only twenty-two years old—we were looking forward to the next fifty or sixty years to be together. We were young and carefree, and all the enticing joys of life were spread before us like a banquet just waiting for us to partake of the good things it offered us. Yet the only thing that mattered in the end was the eternal—our relationship with Him.

Why is it that so many people choose to sample the variety of pleasures of this life, ignoring the eternal because it's "so far away" or "there's plenty of time for that later"? How do they know that? And even if we do have fifty or sixty good years ahead of us, why do we wait one more minute to follow Him when every day could be fresh and new with His joy right now? Even through the pain, we can be joyful when we choose Jesus. When we trust Him, the fruit of His spirit becomes alive in our lives. He actually becomes our life. As Paul said, "To live is Christ...to die is gain."

Matt is experiencing the gain. And I rejoice with him. In the months following his death, I saw how the loving God who allowed me to experience a rich and beautiful love with such a wonderful man drew me into an even deeper, richer relationship with Himself. Regularly, I allowed my pen to speak for my heart as I poured out my inner self on paper. My journal became my love letters to God, and sometimes to Matt.

May 31

These past few days I have walked through the fields and by the ponds where Matt grew up, the place that once echoed with Matt's laughter, the place he loved so much—home.

It is peaceful here, as it is in my heart, for I know that Matt is home now. Though he longed to come back here and be with his family and friends, his greatest desire was to please the Lord.

Through his struggle with cancer, he adopted two verses as his life theme. "According to my earnest expectation and my hope that I will not be put to shame in anything, but that with all boldness, Christ even now as always, will be exalted in my body whether by life or by death. For to me to live is Christ and to die is gain" (Philippians 1:20-21).

This experience is the hardest thing I've ever had to go through. But God has promised me strength and comfort to face what is now and what lies ahead. Jesus is with me, and Matt is with Jesus.

I know, too, that all the love I gave him was special, but it does not compare to the depth of love he's receiving now from our Heavenly Father.

Matt is happy. He has a new life. He can sing again, and he is not suffering. But I'm sure the single thing that makes Matt the happiest is being in the very presence of our Lord.

We will all miss Matt—no one more than I. Yet he will always be with us through our special memories. I will see him again someday when I go to be with Jesus. And though I miss him badly now, I am thankful that I don't have to watch him hurt any more.

He fought a good fight; he finished his course; he kept the faith. Now he's claiming his prize.

I can't imagine the thrill it was for him as he passed from my arms into the loving arms of our God. But I believe he was met with these words: "Well done, good and faithful servant...enter into the joy of the Lord."

It was a Sunday, hot and humid, but still the birds sang sweetly as the preacher said the closing prayer at the graveside service. Surrounding the fresh, dark mound of earth were over a thousand people. Twice that number had been at the funeral service earlier. Obviously, the memory of this man of outstanding character would be forever impressed on the hearts of those who loved him.

"Friends are friends forever if the Lord's the Lord of them...." Matt's friend Tim ended the service with a song that was dear to Matt. Matt had sung it often before at parting times—the close of a school year, the end of a term of summer missions, graduation. Yet now this song took on a fresh new meaning. Although Matt was no longer my husband, we would share a precious bond through Christ for all eternity! The reality of that truth was clear, but I still had a lot of pain to go through before I could really experience the joy.

June 1

They buried Matt yesterday. I don't know what to say. I wanted to write about it then, but it was too painful, and the depth of emotions I have felt this past week has left me physically drained.

Lord, replace the pain and hurt with happy memories and thoughts of Matt's joy being fulfilled in Christ. Then fill me with Your love. You have carried me so far....

Thank You for the quiet moments this morning as I walked to Matt's grave. He's not there, though. It's just a place in memory of him.

You have sustained me, Lord. I'm trusting You to guide each step of the way. May my love for You and my love for Matt cause me to take action, to put feet to my prayers.

I love you both—always.

P.S. You are first, Lord.

As reality slowly found its way through my shield of numbness, my heart ached with a pain I had never experienced before. Thinking about Matt's absence—not only was he not there, he would never be there again—caused me to miss him terribly.

My only comfort came from the thought that God really does work for the best. Matt was so much happier, and I would see him again one day. Meanwhile, I had to try to enjoy life as he did and live each day for Christ.

As I thought about Matt's abundant life, I was overwhelmed at the gift that God had given me in this man. Choosing to be grateful for what I had instead of lamenting what I didn't have, I thanked God for picking me out to share that difficult and heart-wrenching—yet precious and powerful—experience with such a beautiful man. I was determined to never forget what God had taught me through Matt.

As much as I wanted to apply the valuable lessons of life I was learning, the pain in my heart sometimes surged through my entire body, draining my energy and weakening my will.

June 4

Matt,

A constant ache in my heart cuts through my whole being. It's the pain of separation, of never again being able to love you as I did here on earth, never again being able to touch you and hug you.

I've felt this pain before because we've been apart a lot through our short relationship. But it was always with the hope of being together again, of one day becoming one and consummating our love for each other...which we did.

Never before has this pain been so deep, so hurting. I'll never see you or love you the way I used to on this earth. That thought breaks my heart.

There will never be another like you, Matt. You were the best, the very best, and I'm so sad that you're gone.

For you I am happy. I can rejoice in knowing that you will never shed another tear, you will never feel another pain; you will only know the joy of the Lord, of being in His presence day after day.

Please come see me in my dreams, Matt. Your memory is still very much alive here, but I want just to see how happy you are. You didn't look or feel so great when you left us.

Oh, how I wish you had shared the heavy burden that was on your heart those last several weeks. You were so down and heavy-hearted. And as much as I wanted to lift you out of those dark clouds, I could not. I'm glad you are happy now.

I loved you the best way I knew how, Matt. And I will always love you. Forever.

Love, Lisa

Matt continued to occupy my thoughts. My heart was so heavy at times and I felt like it would literally break from the pain of being without him. I could smile and even laugh when I remembered the good times, but the pain still lingered.

And yet God was there to hold me, and it is only in His Word that I could find rest. I was assured of His control, and in that I found peace. I knew He had a plan. I wanted to learn to live again, to rejoice in each new day, to grab hold of God's plan for me and live it! Yet I knew I had to be patient, to let myself heal. It was the time for me to "be still and know." In the stillness I could find rest, because it was in the stillness that I grew in the knowledge that He is God. But it was also in the stillness—and in the busyness—of the days that I continued to be reminded of Matt.

June 6

In everything I see and everywhere I go I find something that reminds me of you, Matt. I hold back tears so many times, saving them until I'm alone in a quiet place. Like now. It hurts. Only God, in time, can heal these deep wounds.

I loved you, Matt, more than I've ever loved anybody before. I can't believe you're gone—you've attained the precious hope of every believer—heaven!

Lord, please grant me patience with myself as I try to recover from the most difficult thing I've ever faced. Thank You that I'm not facing it alone. You are here with me, Lord. And we can make it together.

Lord, I have a very special request—please let me see a vision of Matt as he is now or something that I can understand about him now, in my dreams or thoughts.

Today was such a beautiful day. I can't imagine what heaven will be like. And I can't wait to get there!

I spent a lot of time reading God's Word for encouragement and His promises that we would survive this grief together. Several verses seemed to jump right off the pages of my Bible.

"And I heard a loud voice from the throne saying, 'Now the dwelling of God is with men, and He will live with them. They will be His people, and God Himself will be with them and be their God. He will wipe every tear from their eyes. There will be no more death or mourning or crying or pain, for the old order of things has passed away.' He who was seated on the throne said, 'I am making everything new!'" (Revelation 21:3-5).

In the months following Matt's death, I looked for my "vision." It has since occurred to me that the vision I have seen and continue to see is quite different from what I had hoped to see. It is not really a visible vision—it is God Himself revealing to me more of who He is, allowing me to know Him more and more intimately. In ways I had never before imagined, our creative God, faithful to His Word, showed Himself to me.

"Call to me and I will answer you and tell you great and unsearchable things you do not know" (Jeremiah 33:3).

Looking back, I can see how He was often revealing more about His nature and character through people, through His creation, through whatever means He chose. The Light of the world was continuing to brighten my life, in spite of the deep hurts and frustrations.

June 7

Today has been better and brighter. I read a beautiful poem by Helen Steiner Rice, and it seemed like Matt was speaking directly to me.

When I must leave you
for a little while,
Please do not grieve
and shed wild tears
And hug your sorrow
to you through the years,
But start out bravely
with a gallant smile;
And for my sake
and in my name
Live on and do
all things the same.
Feed not your loneliness
on empty days,
But fill each waking hour
in useful ways,
Reach out your hand
in comfort and in cheer

And I in turn will comfort you
and hold you near;
And never, never
Be afraid to die,
For I am waiting
for you in the sky!

June 8

I wonder if I will always wonder why Matt died so young. Why we never had time together to live out our dreams. Why we never had the chance to live a "normal" life together. So many questions; no answers. And when I get to the place where I'll be able to have some answers from the Controller of Matt's life and mine, I probably will forget about the questions because I'll be so enthralled by the glory of God.

Teach me to be satisfied with Jesus alone, Lord God. Sometimes the pain gets so bad—only You can fill me with your peace and joy.

Thank You for Your comfort, Lord.

June 9

I've been reading through Matt's journals and it makes me feel so close to him—like I know him better and better. Somehow it's like reliving his life with him. Oh, how I wish he were here.

I miss you so badly, Matt. But I know you wouldn't trade heaven for anything in this old world—not even me. I feel sad. I guess I feel cheated, too. Matt, you're the only guy I've ever really loved, the only one in this world I would want to spend my life with. Why did God want you to die? Sometimes I think I'm doing okay. But deep down inside, I have a broken heart.

Teach me, Lord, to cherish special memories, but to go on with life as You would have me to do. Time is too short.

While visiting a friend at Clemson, I was surprised to learn about another young widow. Jamie mentioned that a friend of hers had gone through an experience similar to Matt's and mine. This woman's husband had died of cancer eight months earlier—just two years after they were married. As I asked Jamie what her friend's name was, my emotions tumbled with a diversity of feelings as I found out that she was also a friend of mine.

Understanding what she had been through, I felt sadness and pain for her. Yet at the same time, I experienced a sense of relief and happiness. Here was someone who could really relate, someone who could sincerely share the depths of pain I was going through.

Before Jenny and I ever even talked, I sensed a kindred spirit with her. It's strange how suffering and pain can cause us to cut through the superficial layers of friendship and create bonds of support and understanding. Now God was providing me with such a friend, a friend I had already known.

In 1983, my sister Sandy had been a summer missionary in Florida. Also serving as a summer missionary was an energetic blonde with an easy smile and bright eyes. Sandy and Jenny met at a missions orientation seminar at the start of the summer, and their relationship clicked.

I was preparing to go to college and was anticipating meeting new friends at Clemson University. When Sandy came home, she told me about Jenny, who was a student at Clemson. Sandy said I ought to look her up and get to know her.

The first week at Clemson, I found Jenny at the Baptist Student Union. We became friends and enjoyed each other's company. But Jenny graduated the next semester, and neither Sandy nor I kept in touch with her.

Yet here she was in my life again, and I knew our friendship was not a coincidence. I got her phone number from Jamie and called her that night.

What a blessing to finally talk with someone who could really understand! Sure, a lot of other people had offered their sympathy, and I truly appreciated their expressions of genuine concern. But here was someone who had walked through a similar valley, who knew firsthand what I was going through, someone who could offer comfort in a way no one else had been able to.

I thought of the verses of Psalm 23, "The Lord is my Shepherd, I shall lack nothing.... Even though I walk through the valley of the shadow of death, I will fear no evil, for You are with me; Your rod and Your staff, they comfort me" (vv. 1, 4). Jenny and I could identify with each other, and together we shared how we were learning to trust our Shepherd to guide us, to provide for us all we needed to walk through the valleys.

We spoke with each other only a few more times, but those conversations of comfort and encouragement were a real blessing. Like Paul, I rejoiced in God's faithfulness: "Praise be to the God and Father of our Lord Jesus Christ, the Father of compassion, the God of all comfort, who comforts us in all our troubles, so that we can comfort those in any trouble with the comfort we ourselves have received from God. For just as the sufferings of Christ flow over into our lives, so also through Christ our comfort overflows" (2 Corinthians 1:3-4).

Though this valley I was walking through seemed dark and lonely, I knew I was never alone. In the silence and stillness of my pain, God continued to remind me of His great love.

June 11

I have an exhilarating feeling inside of being loved. Thank You, Lord, for loving me, and thank You for allowing Matt the chance to love me and me to love him. I know this feeling will leave me, but the fact of Your love, and Matt's love, remain....

Thank You for the precious memories I have of Matt. We shared something so wonderful, so precious, so unique.

Lord, open my eyes to see as You see. I want to see Your will so clearly in my life. I want to get serious about living for You now! There's so little time. I can't—I mustn't—waste it! Show me....

Every day was different and brought with it new feelings and thoughts. Some days I felt warm and loved and excited about what the Lord held for me. Other days, my mind focused on the separation and loneliness of being without my precious husband. Learning how to deal with this mixture of feelings challenged my faith. But trusting the Lord to be faithful to His word created a freshness in my relationship with Jesus.

I took special note of the promises I found in my daily Bible readings, and held those promises close to my heart. "And surely I will be with you always" (Matthew 28:20). "I will never leave you or forsake you.... Do not let this Book of the Law depart from your mouth; meditate on it day and night, so that you may be careful to do everything written in it.Then you will be prosperous and successful. Have I not commanded you? Be strong and courageous. Do not be terrified; do not be discouraged, for the Lord your God will be with you wherever you go" (Joshua 1:5, 8-9).

The Lord God had said these things. And although there was no way I could know what would happen if I truly believed what He said, I chose to try Him, to take Him at His word. And I began to see that my own feelings had no effect on the truth of God's word. In spite of the way I felt at times, in spite of the loneliness and the pain and the frustration, my faith caused me to hold strongly to the One true foundation—Jesus Christ, the only One who is "the same yesterday and today and forever" (Hebrews 13:8).

Though my faith was growing stronger with each passing day, I still missed Matt. I missed the romance and the intimate friendship of our relationship. No one could touch me or hug me or kiss me or even look at me the way Matt could. I remembered how it felt to be in his arms—safe, secure, loved. I could never be in Matt's arms again, but I knew I could rest confidently in the Lord's arms. Safe, secure, and loved.

A few weeks after the funeral, I had Matt's family and some of our friends over for dinner at the old house. Matt and I had grown close to Lynne and Jim, and they had become like family. The evening was a time of sweet encouragement. Before they left, Lynne and Jim whispered that they had left a special gift in my bedroom. Expecting an uplifting note or a picture of Matt, I thanked them, and we said our goodbyes.

After the Lockes left, I walked tiredly down the hall to my bedroom. When I walked through the doorway, my eyes opened widely in surprise. There, leaning against my bed, was a guitar wrapped in a nylon case. Beside it was a letter.

Dear Lisa,

Lynne and I have been thinking long and hard as to what we could possibly do for you, and nothing really came to mind.

Then we thought of Matt and how happy he is with Jesus and how happy he always made those around him. We thought about his crazy jokes and his warm heart and his beautiful singing that we will always carry with us, and it finally became evident to us that this is not a time of sorrow, but one of great joy—and you can bet Matt is singing about it.

Together the both of you have given us so much, and there is so much of Matt in you that God has wonderful plans for. One of Matt's greatest testimonies was in his voice, and just as I am sure he is singing now, I know he is happy when you are singing.

We want you to have this guitar so that, should you decide to continue playing, you could maybe make some use of it in continuing Matt's loving testimony and gift of music. He will always be singing with you, and you'll be in our hearts forever.

> *God bless you. Love always,*
> *Jim and Lynne*

A musical instrument seemed a fitting tribute to one who had brought music to so many lives. Matt usually had a song in his heart, and the songs flowed beautifully from his mouth. That guitar became to me a tool of creativity, a therapeutic instrument to aid in working out my feelings, a reminder of the song Jesus longs to sing in all our lives. "He put a new song in my mouth, a hymn of praise to our God. Many will see and fear and put their trust in the Lord" (Psalm 40:3).

How sweet to know the blessings of God and to receive His grace and counsel! With a hungry heart I received the counsel of those who spoke to me with the voice of God. One such person was Dr. Charles Dunn, who had been one of Matt's professors at Clemson. Though I did not know him well, what I knew about him left me with a great deal of confidence in his advice. In a letter he sent to me, he made several points which really caught my attention.

I hope that you will not consider it presumptuous of me to offer a suggestion or two based upon observations I have made of others who have faced crises like yours.

First, I would like to suggest that you not make any major decisions in your life for at least one year, perhaps even longer. So often persons in your situation feel pressured to make major decisions that should be postponed until they can view life with more equanimity.

Second, may I also observe that the trial for you has just begun? As you well know, Satan often leaves us alone while we are going through a great crisis. Then after our moment of triumph, he begins to do his greatest work. You have been shining brilliantly through a great crisis, but in reality a far greater crisis is ahead. The temptation may be to relax now or in the near future, but it is more important than ever before to "watch and pray" lest you fall after a time of God's gracious handiwork in your life. The crisis of recent months has been frontal. The crisis to come will be subtle.

Third, let God graciously and gradually unfold His plan for your life. You are young. The God of eternity builds over the long-run, not the short-run of life. Jesus was thirty before He began His great work. Moses was eighty before God called him to lead the children of Israel. We live in an age that pressures young people to do too much too soon.

Fourth, the Bible tells us to "be still and know that I am God." You will be tempted to become very active, and indeed, well-intentioned friends will encourage you to do so. Activity will not allay the heartache of the present hour; only drawing nigh to God will accomplish this. A crowded calendar of activities is no substitute for close communion with the Almighty.

Fifth, God has not been graciously taking you through this tragic but triumphant crisis if He did not expect more from you later in life. If you have not done so, please read about the life of Elisabeth Elliot, whose husband Jim was martyred by the Auca Indians. She lives today to write and speak around the world. **Through Gates of Splendor** *and* **Shadow of the Almighty** *are the books that I suggest you read.*

Sixth, make sure you have one or two very strong Christian friends whose counsel can be trusted, because "without counsel purposes are disappointed" and "in the multitude of counselors there is safety." Counsel of wise and seasoned Christians will become more important than ever before as you begin to go through this next crisis.

Seventh, remember the great truths of Hebrews 12:1-3, "Therefore, since we are surrounded by such a great cloud of witnesses, let us throw off everything that hinders and the sin that so easily entangles, and let us run the race marked out for us. Let us fix our eyes on Jesus, the author and perfecter of our faith, who for the joy set before him endured the cross, scorning its shame, and sat down at the right hand of the throne of God. Consider him who endured such opposition from sinful men, so that you will not grow weary and lose heart."

Along with many other people, my family continues to pray for you.

To me, this letter was more than just another condolence card or "we're thinking about you." I have read it over and over again, and even today its truths remain imprinted in my life.

As I thought more and more about Matt, I began to reflect on our short relationship. I remembered every detail of our meeting, our dating, our breakup, of getting back together, of our wedding, of our months together as he battled the cancer. My heart was heavy because I didn't think I had adequately communicated my love to him. I read through some of the love letters I had written to Matt, and they seemed so shallow in comparison to the depth of love I felt for him. The tears rolled down my cheeks.

Tears are precious gifts, and I knew my tears were more than just a display of emotion. They expressed my heartfelt cry, releasing whatever was jumbled up inside of me. When I did not understand what I was feeling, when I could not adequately capture my thoughts in my journal, I knew I could cry to the Lord. And He understood my tears.

June 18

It's raining outside and I'm crying inside. Slow, silent tears fill my eyes. It's not for you that I weep, Matt. It's for me. All my life I've waited and watched for the man of my dreams to become real and step into my life. It was so miraculous the way the Lord brought you my way. Actually, He brought me to you. And I am so thankful. Our time together was so short, but so rich, such a blessing....

It hurts to think that our time here is over and the Lord wants me to move on, to keep going. But God, I want to do everything You have set aside for me to do. Teach me and show me. I am still.

Lord, fill this temple of Yours with something beautiful. I'm trusting You to use me—to take me as I am and shape me into a usable vessel through which Your love can flow.

The pain was real, but so was the truth of the Lord's presence with me. How comforting to trust in an ever-present Savior! I knew He would continue to be with me.

I decided to spend a few weeks in Alabama, but it felt strange to be back in my hometown. Nobody there knew Matt very well, and few were close to the situation. Yet hundreds of people had been praying for us and were continuing to pray for me. I thought it might be easier for me to be there, but it reminded me of the previous summer. I felt like I should be planning our wedding instead of grieving over Matt's death. What drastic changes had taken place in my life in one short year! *One day,* I kept thinking, *one day I'll feel normal again. I am okay. I know I'm okay. And one day I'm going to feel okay.* I found comfort and strength from holding on to the Lord.

June 20

Lord, You are my strength and shield. No good thing will You withhold from those who love You. I love You, Lord. And I want to obey You and look for and receive every blessing You have for me.

Thank You, Lord, for Your love. Your grace is greater than my need. Your love reaches deeper than the depth of my pain. Your joy overwhelms my sorrow.

I can sing, for I am free in Christ...to love, to live, to give—to be all that I can be for Christ Jesus, my Lord.

Father, help me to put away childish things, to forget what is past and to reach toward the prize of the upward call in Christ Jesus. Thank You for seeing my pain, for comforting me in my sorrow.

I want to thank You again and again for the chance that Matt and I had to love each other. We were so fulfilled—some people never taste such satisfaction and joy in many decades of marriage. I love You. Keep strengthening me. I am weak.

June 22

Oh, Matt, you were so wonderful, so good to me. I miss you, but you are at rest. You are truly happy, and I would never ask you to come back here to face the pain of life on earth. Your joy is complete in Jesus—and so is mine. The days are long without you.

Lord, continue to fill the loneliness and emptiness that is so much a part of me now. Oh, God, it hurts so badly to be without him. Thank You that You won't ever leave me. You are always here. Hold me close to You, Jesus. I want my life to be filled with the fruit of the Spirit.

Please direct my thinking, Lord. Give me a small glimpse of my Home. I can't wait to get there. I love You!

Love, Lisa

Often in my moments alone with God, I strummed and picked the strings of my guitar, singing to my Heavenly Father. I found a sanctuary in worshiping the Lord with the music He had given me. One quiet summer night in June, I sat alone in the den of my parents' home. Picking a tune I had composed, I focused my mind and heart on what it was like for me to watch my husband to pass on from death to a new life. Slowly and sweetly, lyrics began to flow with the tune I was playing. Alone with God, I sang it to Matt. It would be a while before I was able to share it with anyone else.

As I watched you breathing
Your last suffering breath,
Thoughts of Jesus would comfort me,
His glory would be shown in your death.

You were drawn from my arms
To the loving arms of our God,
And I know He said, "Well done, my child.
A faithful path you have trod."

And though my heart hurts—
I miss your presence here—
I'm so very thankful
That Jesus is always so near.

His love, oh His wondrous love
Reaches deeper than all of my pain,
And I understand my loss on earth
Is nothing but heaven's sweet gain.

Now I look forward
To seeing your precious smile once again,
But greater to see Jesus,
And to hear Him say, "Enter in."

Yes, we'll be together again,
Together, forever, in Him.

Each time I sang the song, I was brought back to that hospital room at NIH, back to the bedside of my dying husband. I relived the experience of letting go. And somehow, each time I thought more deeply about what it must have been like for God to let go of His perfect Son at that moment that Jesus bore all of our sins on the cross. Several weeks later, another song took form within my heart and mind.

As I watched You breathing
Your last suffering breath,
I had to turn my face away
You bore the weight of sin in your death.

Perfect Lamb, blameless One,
Man—yet divine—You are God;
A life of love and obedience,
A faithful path You had trod.

Does mankind understand this?
The greatest act of love ever shone—
My Son became a sacrifice
So those who believe would become My own.

God-Incarnate, Jesus Christ,
I chose to become a man,
Through the cross I conquered sin
According to My perfect plan.

Now I look forward
To the joy that lies beyond the cross;
My power will resurrect My life in You—
My Son, in Your death there is no loss.

Oh, what joy in this triumph!
This victory we have won!
And so now it is finished,
And yet we've only just begun.

Everything is Yours, My precious Son.
No one else could ever do what You have done.

The thought was overwhelming—*no one else* could have done what Jesus did for us. He did all that needed to be done for us to have an intimate relationship with our God, for redemption of sin, for restoration of real life, real love. Now He was teaching me how to claim what was mine as a new creation in Him. Through the sorrow and the sadness, through the pain and the hurting, I could still have an abundant, joy-filled life! I could find deeper meaning in the things that mattered in life—eternal things, the Word of God. Each day His reality was breaking through to me, and though the pain was great, I discovered His love and goodness were greater still.

Yes, there would be scars, but they were beautiful reminders of His healing and His work in my life. He had planned for me a life full of adventure and dreams. I believed that whatever God had in store for me, this pain, these scars, were just part of the preparation.

Then I began to realize something very important. God was calling me to be conformed to the image of Christ. Only He knew what was necessary to create that image in me. Was anything else of more value? No. I knew that God must have the freedom in our lives to do what He needs to do to accomplish His purpose in us. For me, the pain and the scars were not part of the preparation; they were part of the process God used to continue the good work He had already begun in me.

Matt and I had dreamed many times of heading west on an adventurous vacation someday. We never had the opportunity to make the trip, but I decided to hold on to that dream. My two sisters and a roommate from college set out on an adventure with me. Though I dearly missed Matt, the trip was therapeutic and exhilarating. I was able to visit many special friends and see places I had never seen before. We experienced a bounty of God's beauty.

July 2

We had a busy day today...it was really tiring. It seems that everything is only half the fun without Matt. It's not as easy to laugh and have a good time and be funny without him. But those are not life's most important things anyway. Suffering, patience, trials, perseverance—those are the companions that will cause me to grow to be like Jesus.

On the Fourth of July we camped out at the Grand Canyon. After pitching our two-man tent, the four of us went exploring. I was excited, seeing the same wonder and beauty that Matt saw when he was a summer missionary there, seeing the places he had spoken and written about. I missed him even more, realizing once again that he was gone forever, that he would never again be with me here on earth. But then I sensed a new joy of knowing he was in heaven with Jesus, and that I, too, would be there one day.

July 4

Oh, thank You, God, for this very special experience. All these feelings and emotions wrapped up in one little me, mastered by one big You! I love You, Lord. Thanks for the assurance that I am in Your hands and that You love me—You will what is best...my will yielded to Yours.

I viewed the canyon in all of its splendor. It was little more than a deep valley with high, steep sides. At the bottom of those firm, silent walls of rock flowed a river alive with motion and sound. The river had cut through the rock leaving deep, deep scars, like the deep scars in my own life. And at the center of my being flowed a river of living water. God's handiwork here before me—and in my own life—was beautiful! I claimed yet another promise: "Whoever believes in Me, as the Scripture has said, streams of living water will flow from within Him" (John 7:38).

On "the adventure" with my sisters Becky (left) and Sandy (right)

God was evidently working in my life. He was consistently Himself, faithful and true. I, however, was not so consistent. Often it seemed as if my emotions were in conflict with my faith, when in reality they were a part of my faith. If there had not been such a rich love, there would not be such deep pain. My sadness turned me to the Lord and caused me to hold on to Him more strongly.

July 5

Oh, God! My heart has been torn in two: one part is here ...the other is safe with You. Thank You for that!
I know the verses. I know the words of comfort. I know that everything will be all right, even though my heart says everything is all wrong. You are the only

*One who can help me deal with it. Direct me in all that
I do, Lord Jesus. I willingly submit to You.*

July 6

My dearest Matt,
*I can't wait to be where you are. Oh, how exciting
to be in the very presence of Jesus! You must be singing
praises and dancing for joy and "fellowshiping." Won't
it be wonderful when we're all there together?*

July 8

*Lord God, You are amazing! I can't wait to see
what You have in store. You are filling me with Your
love and power. You are nurturing me and
strengthening me to carry on the message that Matt so
loudly proclaimed with his life. You are Love! Show me
how and where You want me—I don't ever want to take
a step out of Your will. I want to learn all You want to
teach me. I want to share all You have given me to
share. Thank You, Jesus. You are my forever friend and
Lord of my life.*
*Thank You, Jesus, for what was, what is, and what
is to come. You are the Lord and Master of all of it. You
are the Guide and Director of real life.*
*You blessed me bountifully with our marriage; You
continue to strengthen me and nurture me now that he
is home with You and I'm left on earth; You have hid
my life "in Christ with God." My life is in Your hands.
Thank You! May my life be a reflection of Your glory.*

Love, Lisa

We made it back safely from our "adventure." But I still wasn't sure what to expect being back in Alabama. Many times I just sat still and relived memories.

July 12

So strange. Coming home, but not to him.... I had some mail waiting, but none from him. There are lots of pictures and cards and letters from the past. But I so want Matt here now. I want to be with him again. To touch him, to love him—I dream of being beside him forever.

Lord, help me to face each new day with Your strength and Your love—sometimes I feel like I don't have any of my own. Thank you for my family—they have been such a good support for me, more than I even realize.

I want to begin praying now about the books I will write. I want them to be inspired by You alone. You are my treasure.

Yours, Lisa

It was strange not being identified with Matt any longer. My "place" had been as Matt's wife, yet I knew that my security was not in him. I had to find my security in Jesus Christ. I had to continually yield to Him. He was becoming to me all He said He would. I kept track of these unfolding revelations in my journal.

July 13

Yielded to You
    for You are my life
You are my strength
    through suffering and strife
You are my peace
    through struggles and unrest
You are my joy
    You know what's best
You are my love
    and You're preparing
My eternal home
    which is beyond comparing
Oh, to see You one day
    face to face!
And to live in the light of
    Your eternal grace
I am ready and listening
    for the trumpet call
For now and always
    I give You my all.

In yielding to God, in choosing to take Him at His word, my faith was being stretched. Though I felt a wide range of emotions—emptiness, frustration, happiness, impatience, pain—I believed that God's Word was true and I trusted Christ to work all things together for my good. No matter what I felt, the truth of Jesus rose above all else. I needed Him to be foremost in my life.

July 14

I feel so ugly and full of pain. There is an emptiness in me today. I haven't let Jesus fill me like only He can. I have drifted through the day without much thought of Christ's sacrifice for me.

Forgive me, Lord. You died so that I might really live. Help settle my soul and provide clear direction for my life so that I will learn how to live. I need Your guidance. Teach me how to draw closer to You. I love You!

Lord, share with me this burden of loneliness, of being without my best friend on earth. I see things every day that remind me of what he was to me.... You grew us through all the struggles and turned the ugliness into something beautiful, something good. Help me to share the message of Your love to a dying world. That sounds like an old cliché! But I want it to be truth...agape love in my life every day.

July 16

I really feel like a widow right now...it's like a sudden wave of reality—Matt is gone, and he's not coming back.

I feel so sentimental. I want to look at all his pictures, read all the love letters again, relive all the good times.... I've been filling my head with other thoughts when I really need to let Jesus fill my life.

God, only You can fill the emptiness. I want to be filled with Your holiness and purity. I want my life to count for the kingdom, today—forever!

July 19

It's lonely. The "empty" still persists. Not so much empty in my heart, for the Lord has filled me with His love—but empty in my actions, my thoughts, my head. I

*have noticed an awkwardness in the way I behave
sometimes.*

*Lord Jesus, I am nothing—You are all
I want to follow when You call
Tune my ears to You alone
Direct my life which You own
May my eyes seek Your face
And I will surely find the place
That You have patterned just for me
That's where I always want to be.*

*Thank You, Lord, for saving me from ugly sin and
a life doomed to hell. I owe You all that I am. I want my
entire being to focus on You.*

My sister Sandy and I came to know Christ about the same time—I was seven years old; she was eight. Growing up we were more than sisters; we were friends.

Throughout high school and college we had different circles of friends and activities, yet there was always the special bond of sisterhood. Now as I was grieving and growing through pain, my sister was sensitive and quietly supportive with her prayers, words of encouragement, and hugs. She invited me to spend a week with her at her apartment.

Sandy and I attended a Bill Gothard seminar that week. I hoped for good fellowship as well as deeper discoveries in God's Word. We were like sponges, soaking up all we could about biblical principles and the application of those principles in everyday life.

Clearly, I begin to realize afresh that my security was rooted in Christ alone. Though I felt my life had hit bottom, I found out that bottom was solid with Christ as my foundation. I knew then that whatever God called me to do, whatever He would choose for me to go through, we could make it together. He would not allow anything in my life that He had not already provided for. My heart burned to know my Lord better.

July 21

Oh, God, I want my life to be consumed by my passion for You. Create in me a spirit of reverence, of gratefulness.... Let me be submissive to You alone during this time of adjustment and transition

It's hard to be "one" again, with just You and me—instead of You and Matt and me. But he is with You now, Lord, safe and secure, so, so happy. That's where he's always wanted to be. I long to be there, too.

Show me how to use what You have brought me through. Open doors that only You can open and lead me boldly through them to new blessings, new ministries. Your work is what my life is all about.

I give You all my rights, whatever possessions I have referred to as "mine," and all that I am. Empty me of myself that I may be filled with You alone. Take everything, God, and use what You will for Your glory.

A new excitement was taking over my life. The Lord Jesus Christ captivated me and began to give me glimpses of the abundant life He offers all of us—a life of peace, of joy, of hope bound together by His love. I needed Him.

As I came to know more about the holy and righteous God to whom I had committed my life, I became increasingly aware of my nothingness, of the depravity of my sinful nature. I wanted Him to become my all.

The biblical principles I had learned at the Bill Gothard seminar kept running through my mind. Paul asked in 1 Corinthians 6:19-20, "Do you not know that your body is a temple of the Holy Spirit, who is in you, whom you have received from God? You are not your own; you were bought with a price. Therefore honor God with your body."

I began to see that my life was not really mine after all. Not only had my Lord God created me, but Jesus had bought me back with the sacrifice of His life. I was determined to live for Him, not for myself.

One thing the seminar emphasized that deeply impressed me was the importance of the Word itself. God speaks to His children through His Word. And by meditating on that Word, I could establish His truths in my mind and my heart. It became my goal to personalize the Scripture, to let God's Word be my words, to encourage others with His Word, and to speak to Him in the language of His Word.

My heart became hungry to know Him more and to be filled only with Him. As I became empty of my selfishness, I could delight in Jesus Christ and let Him show me what it was He wanted me to do.

I was also learning to experience God's peace. "Peace I leave with you; my peace I give you. I do not give to you as the world gives. Do not let your hearts be troubled and do not be afraid" (John 14:27). It was a precious gift that I gladly accepted.

What a blessing that week was! Not only had I experienced a deeper realization of His love and faithfulness; I had also enjoyed a special time with my sister. She was becoming one of my best friends. Spiritually, socially, physically—we had grown up together. I returned to my parents' home more strongly bonded to my sister and to my Lord.

July 27

Two months since Matt died—it seems so far away and long ago since I've seen him.... We can never be together again physically, but sometimes I feel like our spirits are communing.

(Matt, I miss you, darling. I yearn for you, for your presence here. I long to see your smile and to hear your voice....)

Oh, Lord, save me from this pain and sorrow. Help me to grieve and work through the hurting. Take my hand and lead me through to the light, Your light. I want to see Jesus.

Help me apply the many things I'm learning through trials and suffering. You have given me a new ministry, Lord; I am not worthy of it except through the blood of Christ.

My heart hurts tonight. Heal me, Lord Jesus.

July 29

Thank You, Lord, for freedom! You've given us freedom from sin through Your death. For the first time tonight I thought about what it must have been like for Jesus to be out of fellowship with God at the one moment when the Father turned His face away—how horrifying! Yet so necessary. A holy God cannot look on the sins of the world as Jesus was bearing them. Thank You—I am forever grateful, for my life, to You alone.

My body is exhausted. So is my mind. My spirit, however, can soar on the wings of Christ's love for me. Thank You for the little things You do, Lord, that show Your love for me—a perfect, unconditional love.

It hurts to think about those last few days of Matt's life. The pain, the helplessness, the utter despair.

Knowing he was leaving, but not being able to talk with him about it because his head wasn't clear....

But now the peace, the joy of knowing he's experiencing God's great love and companionship in person—as I will. He entered into the joy of the Lord.

Help me to understand Your ways better, Lord. But first I must obey. Trust and obey.

One of Matt's nurses had given us Hannah Hurnard's book *Hind's Feet on High Places*. I was captivated by the story of little "Much-Afraid." It seemed to be about me—Much-Afraid, whose companions were Suffering and Sorrow, on her journey to the High Places.

Often she was attacked by fear and pride and all sorts of evil relatives who tried to get her to turn back. But she was persevering, even though the way sometimes got dark and stony. There were rough places that caused her to stumble. There were times when she thought she'd like to take an easier route. But through the Shepherd's gentle leading and teaching, she learned there were no short cuts to obedience. Following the will of the Shepherd became her greatest desire, so she laid everything on the altar to obey Him. Oh, how I wanted to do the same with my life! To go to the High Places I had to walk with Suffering and Sorrow for a while.

Along her journey, Much-Afraid developed hind's feet and would eventually bound to the High Places. Also, her name was changed—to "Acceptance-with-Joy."

So what about *my* journey to the "High Places"? I was confident of my destination, but I had questions about the way I was going to get there.

August 5

God, I feel so blank right now. My life is open and there doesn't seem to be much there...except You.

What is really going on? Am I growing stronger through this pain or am I denying that it exists? Have I reached a new plateau of being secure and happy or am I hiding what's really deep down inside?

So many people tell me what it was like for them to grieve, to work through their suffering. Is it so very different for me that I have resolved my grief through the Lord's perfect love and peace?

Before the weekend that would have been our first anniversary, I decided to take a short trip and visit some friends. My first stop was in Birmingham, to stay with my friend Kelly. We reminisced about our college days and about Matt. One year Kelly had been a contestant in the Miss Clemson pageant, and Matt had been asked to sing as part of the evening's entertainment.

It was a great night for Kelly—she was named first runner-up. Matt's night, however, was less of a success.

When he walked out on stage for his solo, he had to stand in the spotlight for several minutes before the stage crew could get the piano and music set up. Standing in the middle of the stage with nothing to do but smile, Matt humbly received the whistles and catcalls from the audience. The moments of waiting for the piano music to start apparently unnerved him. As he made his way through the first verse, a puzzled expression suddenly came over his face. He couldn't remember the words, so he hummed through the last few bars. The chorus sounded great with Tim, the piano player, singing harmony. When the cue for the second verse came around, another panic-stricken expression returned to Matt's face. No words came.

"Now, I'm not gonna do this!" he said, frustrated. "Tim!"

But Tim kept right on going, and eventually Matt caught up with him. He maintained his composure and finished out the song, then nearly ran off the stage. It was real entertainment for the audience, but Matt was more than a little embarrassed. As we remembered that night and other memories, Kelly and I laughed. Being able to relive the old days with my friends—Matt's friends, too—was precious. Even in the midst of grief, there is a special joy in sharing memories of the one who died.

Kelly's mom and I shared tears as she told me of a painful time in her life. When her son was a baby, he had to have several surgeries to correct a bone problem. Even those long-ago memories of watching him suffer and being helpless to relieve the pain caused her to cry. I knew those feelings. Tears rolled down my cheeks as I related what I felt in watching my husband's physical pain—the feelings of frustration, helplessness, heartache.

It was stormy the next afternoon as I left to continue my trip. I listened to the music of the rain and sang along with it as I drove. My spirit was singing, too. I knew Jesus was my constant companion, and I was thankful for those people He had brought into my life to share this special time.

Mike and Becky were good friends of Matt's. Although I didn't know them at Clemson, our friendship grew through Matt. He had also introduced me to a girl named Melanie, and our friendship had become something precious. As we all met at Mike and Becky's, I knew we would have a joyful time. I would even be able to laugh heartily as we played silly games and talked about fun times, special memories, and Matt.

Mike's father had died suddenly of a heart attack several years earlier, so they knew about mourning and grieving. Mike's mother had some of her journal entries published into a beautiful book entitled *Walking into Morning,* and I was anxious to look through it.

As we sat in the living room talking that evening, I picked up the book and began to scan portions of it. The lump in my throat and tears in my eyes caused me to hurriedly put it down.

Later, when everyone had settled down for the night, I picked up the book again and read it from cover to cover. What an excellent message of one woman's journey through grief! It was a story I could empathize with and be encouraged by. I marveled at how strange and wonderful it was that God could bond together a twenty-three-year-old widow and a forty-year-old widow, how we could share hearts without ever knowing each other. My time with Mike and Becky and Mel was precious, and finding that book was a special, unexpected blessing.

The next morning as I headed back to my parents' home, I thought about how therapeutic it had been to be able to laugh with my friends, sharing memories and making new ones. Grieving was not easy, but through it God had given me His strength when I had none, His hope when I was hopeless, His love when I felt empty. He was filling my heart with Himself.

August 8

I cried many tears today in the quietness of my bedroom closet while I listened to Matt's tapes, then on my mom's shoulder.

So many feelings are jumbled up inside. There was even something about coming back to Florence, to this house, that made me cry.

I can't even begin to write how I feel. I still regret not ever talking to Matt about death...about heaven ...about seeing Jesus. Too much wasted time spent on television, idle chatter, apart.

I don't understand myself today. But You do, Lord. I'm thankful You know what I am feeling. You understand me.

I desperately miss Matt right now. My sweetheart is gone. It's hard to fathom the events of this past year and their repercussions.

I am alone. I am lonely. I am sad. I am hurting. My heart is broken. Yet I can rejoice in the Lord always! Thank You, God, that this earth won't last much longer, but Your Word endures forever, even as we who are born into Your love do.

Tomorrow, if You haven't come back by then, I will need an extra boost of strength.

August 9

Just one year ago today.... Our wedding day was thrilling as we shared our union with friends and family before God. But our wedding night was exhilarating as we shared our love with each other.

Oh, Matt, how I love you! Oh, how I thank the Lord for the opportunity I had to be your wife, your best friend. What a joy to share in every part of your life....

On this day, I miss you terribly. It's the day we couldn't wait to come, so we could say we'd been married a year, then over a year, then a year and a half....

Matt, I know you are ecstatic, and though our bodies and souls cannot be together today, our spirits can always celebrate the joy of the Lord as one in Him.

You are a treasure, Matt. God's treasure. I'm glad the Lord shares His treasures with me.

Thank You, Lord Jesus, for a year of love and pain, of growth and renewal, of aching and hurting ...and healing. I love You, Lord!

Love, Lisa

Matt singing at the Miss Clemson Pageant

"I got married last August, and that's a date I guess I better not forget.... "

His voice, so warm and humble, trailed on, but my thoughts were diverted as I listened to the tape of his testimony. As I sat alone in a quiet place, I was thankful for this chance to listen again to the things he had said on that night more than four months ago.

Pensive, I found myself wondering if there was any way he could remember our anniversary. Would anything special happen to show that Matt, too, was thinking about this day we had become one? My vision blurred as my eyes filled with tears. *Will you remember, Matt?*

Through the pain of my heart, I sensed a quiet anticipation. I could celebrate God's limitless love for me. And I was overwhelmed as God unfolded a beautiful surprise for me.

On August ninth, some dear friends from my parents' church were driving home after evening worship services. I had shared a brief testimony of God's sufficient grace at the service, and Don and Susan were talking about me. They had wanted to do something special for me, and they knew the Lord was directing them to bless me in a special way. He had put the desire in their hearts to give me a gift.

The next day Susan brought me a gift certificate, and I was overwhelmed by the generosity of this couple. The gift certificate was from a local computer store. They had no way of knowing that Matt and I had planned on purchasing a computer when his treatments were completed; we wanted to write a book together about his battle with the cancer and the lessons the Lord taught us through the ordeal, so we had begun saving for what would have been a gift to ourselves.

Not wasting much time, I went the following day to the computer store and talked to the salesman. After describing what I wanted to use the computer for, he named a model that would suit my needs perfectly. They had one left. But the gift certificate was not quite enough to cover the cost. I remembered then, this model was the one Matt and I had planned on purchasing. Somehow I knew this computer was supposed to be mine, and I decided to pay the extra money for it. As I stood there waiting for the clerk to box it up and get a writing program, the thought hit me. *This is my anniversary present! God and Matt got together and chose Don and Susan to give me this very special gift. For His glory!*

A few days later the clerk at the store called to say they had torn up the check I'd written. The couple wanted to pay the entire price. Our giving and loving Lord often brings wonderful surprises.

August 10

The day after. I stood outside and looked at the moon tonight. Shrouded with clouds, the full, pale yellow moon still showed its brightness. That's the way Matt was. Though problems and pressures sometimes crowded in on him, he still reflected Your glory. Isn't that the way it's supposed to be?

Because I was not sure what direction God was taking me (though I knew it was toward Him), I went on with plans Matt and I had made before his illness. I went back to our house to live, back to Pope Drive Baptist Church to worship and be an active part of the fellowship, back to Clemson to pursue another degree. As I drove the four-hundred-mile trip, I played tape after tape of praise music. My heart was full of joy as I sang along with the music, knowing Jesus was taking care of me.

August 11

I'm at Sandy's tonight—on my way back to South Carolina. Back to Honea Path and Clemson. Back to old friends. But not back to Matt. The pain is so very real. He is such a precious treasure—now he is with You ...his treasure.

It's so strange. Going back, but not to him. He was always there when I returned to South Carolina.

Thank You, Lord. Thank You, thank You, thank You, that You chose me to be Matt's wife. I love You!

August 12

When I first returned, a dark depression came over me for a few moments—that feeling of loneliness, yearning for my husband. Memories, memories. Sometimes I wish I could go back in time a year. I would go through all the pain again, just to see him one more time, to talk to him, to hear him laugh, to love him.

But Your spirit lifted that darkness and replaced it with the Light of Jesus' love for me and for Matt. Matt is not here, yet the message of his joyful life lives here; the memories of his childhood years live here, and his love and laughter fill this place he called home for so long. He is at his real home now—his eternal home with You. How I thank You, Lord, for Your promise of life with You—forever. I can't wait to be there some day.

I was glad to be back at the old home, back to Matt's childhood home, but staring me in the face in every nook and cranny of the house were Matt's things—his clothes, books, pictures, keepsakes. For me the best thing was to go ahead and clean out as much as possible. I still wanted to keep pictures of him all through the house. Though the pictures couldn't reveal his personality, they did capture his smile. His happy smile and cheerful radiance made me think of the joy he must know in heaven—and the joy we both know in Jesus.

Cleaning out closets could have been painful drudgery, but God is capable of bringing His light even into the darkest of closets. Still, even in His light there was a sort of quiet eeriness in going through Matt's clothes and deciding what to keep and what to give away.

It took me several days to look through his things. Every box and drawer contained a part of him, and I relived many memories. There was the shirt flaming with bright blue, green, and red Mexican scenes I bought for him on our honeymoon. I remembered the fun I had bartering for it with a pushy shopkeeper at a crowded Cancún marketplace. Some short-and-sweet love notes I had stuck in his lunch bags were stuffed in a box. As I read them I was thankful for the many times I told him or wrote to him that I loved him. His shoes, his favorite cowboy boots, his hats—what would I do with them? It was hard to let go of his things because it was like letting go of him.

I didn't feel like I could keep all of his things; I didn't want to be selfish and cling to too many "reminders" that I knew I would never use. His three brothers were about the same size as Matt, I thought, so I took a bunch of his clothes to the Lockes. It was difficult to take them in—emotional. I could hardly keep from crying. Larry nearly cried, too. Oh! the pain of letting go of one so precious. Yet I could be thankful that One more precious was safely keeping us in His care. "Wait for the Lord; be strong and take heart and wait for the Lord" (Psalm 27:14).

August 18

Why am I here, God? I know many good reasons why I should be. To minister, to show that life can go on, to let Your light shine through me, to proclaim that You are Lord and Shepherd of my heart.

Where do I go from here, Lord? I don't know, but I trust You to show me. I will continue to seek You with all my heart.

I registered at Clemson today. No problems. Saw some people I know. One guy asked me how Matt was. He's fine now...in heaven.

God, give me strength and courage to face what I must at Clemson. Help me to remember that I can do all things through Christ who strengthens me.

August 20

I remember this time about four years ago. I parked in this parking lot and walked to my first class here at Clemson University. So many things have changed since then—here on the campus as well as in my own life.

Lord, thank You for being with me always. I need You so much today. My heart aches....

(later)

I'm sitting amidst the tall slender pines on a small tree stump. The point juts into Lake Hartwell—peaceful blue waters moving quietly with the breeze. Chirps and buzzes from bugs and crickets are the only audible sounds, except for the occasional call of a bird.

I can't see anyone for miles, yet I am not alone. My spirit is refreshed by the beauty of the Lord reflected in this tranquil scene. He leads me beside quiet waters and restores my soul.

Matt and I frequented this spot. To talk, to be alone together, to enjoy the beauty of the place. Thank You for the memories, Lord. I love You.

August 21

It's You and me, God, here in the depths of the library. You have renewed my enthusiasm. You have given me an excitement about this semester. I am seeking You, Lord, and I'm trusting You to broaden my ministry as I deepen my message. Thank You, God. I don't know if what I feel right now will last beyond today, but I'm not even promised a tomorrow. And it only matters that Your love and Your joy and Your care for me are eternal.

Even in the sadness of missing Matt, I was glad to be back at Clemson. I would often go to familiar places in town and on campus to sit and to think, to pray and to wonder at the Lord's ways. Thinking of Matt—smiling, talking, laughing—and things we did together made me happy. And even though I missed his presence with me, when I sat alone in those familiar places I was more aware than ever of the real presence of God. He was with me always.

One of my favorite places to visit was Twelve-Mile Beach, a sandy park on the lake. Even though it was several miles away from Clemson, sun-seeking students poured down to the beach on hot, blue-skied days. I liked to go when the crowds were gone, perhaps on overcast, breezy days, to sit on the picnic tables or climb the monkey bars.

I remembered another August day sitting at Twelve-Mile Beach late one afternoon in August. Matt and I had been apart all summer, he at summer school in Clemson, and I on summer missions in Colorado. When I returned to campus after our summer break, Matt told me of a girl he had grown close to, and he was confused now about our relationship. We were engaged at the time, and he was trying to determine whether or not he should break the engagement. Clouds hung overhead and the choppy waves lapped on the shore—the scene was somewhat reflective of what Matt might have been feeling.

Two years later, I was alone as I drove again to Twelve-Mile Beach.

August 24

There is a nice breeze today, and the brightness of the sun dulls the blue sky. As the water gently and softly laps upon the shore, I am reminded of a few years ago. A time when Matt was struggling with a decision, a decision that included me...or excluded me. Thank You, God, for giving him the wisdom to make the right choice.

And I remember when we came out here to sit in the sun. We tried to study, but to no avail. I miss his companionship, Lord.

God, help me to be patient. Sometimes I get in such a hurry to get on with life, to know where You want me to go and to get there. Help me to remember that the journey is the most important part.

The journey. God was showing me that His plan for my life was not a neatly wrapped package; it was the way I was going, a gradual unfolding of Himself in my life. It was coming to know Him through walking with Him. The choices I would make, the circumstances in which I would find myself, the people in my life—these were all parts of the way I was going. As I was seeking the Truth, I was finding real Life in the Way. "Jesus answered, 'I am the Way and the Truth and the Life. No one comes to the Father except through Me'" (John 14:6).

Sometimes my "way" became more cluttered than I wanted. On top of a forty-five-minute commute to Clemson and my classes each day, I also kept busy with school work, church activities, and friends. I often felt ragged and worn from hectic schedules and a fast-paced lifestyle—quite a change from the slow, quiet summer months. It also seemed that the process of grieving sapped away my emotional energy, leaving me feeling exhausted. Yet I knew I could "do all things through Christ who strengthens me" (Philippians 4:13). He would be my strength when I didn't have any—physically, spiritually, or emotionally.

It was during those times when I was so exhausted I didn't feel like doing anything that I really missed Matt's encouragement and companionship. Deep in my heart was a longing for true companionship. It was a longing I had to let God fill. The pain of Matt's death was too fresh for me to even consider dating, and to tell the truth I was somewhat rebellious toward the very idea. For now and always, Jesus remains my first Love. My greatest satisfaction in life would be found only in loving Him with all my heart, soul, and mind.

"Who shall separate us from the love of Christ? Shall trouble or hardship or persecution or famine or nakedness or danger or sword?...No, in all these things we are more than conquerors through Him who loved us. For I am convinced that neither death nor life, neither angels nor demons, neither the present nor the future, nor any powers, neither height nor depth, nor anything else in all creation, will be able to separate us from the love of God that is in Christ Jesus our Lord" (Romans 8:35, 37-39).

Yes! I believe it. My life is in Christ. Matt's life is in Christ. I thought about his new life and birth into the eternal kingdom as his earthly birthday approached. Would they celebrate his birthday in heaven?

September 3

Happy Birthday, Matt! I can't think of a better place for you to spend your birthday than heaven! God allowed me to feel good today...and then your brother David brought those pictures of you your mom sent, and I felt the pain of being without you—especially today. We never did anything special for your birthday, except be together—that was always special enough for me, just to be by your side. Oh, how I miss your companionship, sweetheart. My darling Matt—I'm so thankful for you, for heaven, for Jesus!

Through my grief, I continued to be amazed at God's presence and His faithfulness. His peace, that wonderful passing-all-understanding peace, filled my life. Even in the jumble of emotional confusion, I could know His peace. Even as my life was moving on, further away from the all-too-brief time Matt and I were together, His peace was real.

Although I was finally realizing that I was supposed to keep on living even though my husband had died, I found myself wanting to hold the memory of Matt close to me, so that he would always be a part of me. I didn't want to "get over" him and move on. You're supposed to "get over" a lost ball game or a broken toy. Rather, I wanted to "grow through" this part of my journey, to realize and apply all the things God desired to teach me through this experience. His Spirit was working in my life, and I did not want to suppress Him. My thoughts went back to Matt's urgent prayer, "Whatever it takes."

As I was growing and grieving, there were moments when no words could describe what was going on inside. Often I asked myself, *Is this what they call grief?* It's such a strange thing. Inside I felt pain and hurt; outside I could smile and chat and "kid around." Yet as a part of me was dying, there was new life springing forth. I couldn't always see it or feel it, but I knew it was there. And then I would ache again and miss my dear husband. How could I go on without him? Only with Jesus as my strength, my guide, my source of love—and life. Yes, I could go on...with Jesus. Only with Him. Only He knew what it took to reproduce Himself in me, and whatever it was costing me seemed to pale in the light of His glory. After all, my pain was helping me to trust Him more.

September 7

God, how can I live the rest of my life without the man I love so much? There is an emptiness in everything I do because he is not here. The source of so much happiness and love is gone from my side. A life that was so good and so beautiful.... But he's even more beautiful now that he is with You. His life continues to be a reflection of Your glory.

My heart hurt today when I opened the thank you note from a precious newlywed couple. I am happy for them—they are so happy! But I am sad for me. I have a difficult time being happy because my husband is not here. He left a void that can be filled by no one. No one? Not now...maybe not ever. Can You do that, Lord? Can You fill the emptiness in my life? I think You're the only One who really can. I need You, Lord. My life is nothing without You. You are my source of strength. And people are noticing You are the power behind my life. Please don't let me or my self-pity get in the way of the beautiful things You are doing in my life. I trust You.

"And the God of all grace, who called you to His eternal glory in Christ, after you have suffered a little

while, will Himself restore you and make you strong, firm and steadfast" (1 Peter 5:10).

Writing down my thoughts and my recollections was a special balm for my spirit, and I kept my journal handy to record what I was going through. My emotions seemed to swing chaotically from depression over losing my best friend to incredible joy at the knowledge that he was at the feet of Jesus, and that I was learning to become closer to our Lord through this experience.

September 10

The sunset painted brilliant colors across the sky, and I had to stop and gaze at God's beautiful creation as I stepped outside in the backyard of my country home. The stillness and beauty of the moment held my attention for a while; then my eye followed the path of the sun. Silhouetted against a background of pinks and blues was a cluster of mimosa trees which had sprung up within the last several months. I remembered the story my husband had told me about the tree he planted from seed when he was a child.

Matt loved the outdoors. He loved dogs and walks and ponds and trees, but most of all he loved the Lord who created every good and perfect thing. It was this love for Christ and from Christ that overflowed to all those who knew him, even as a young boy—when he decided to plant a tree.

He picked out a spot in the backyard, the same backyard I was standing in. He dug a hole and dropped the seed in, and then he waited. He watered and cared for the tree, and soon it grew. It became a beautiful tree with friendly branches that waved to all who played nearby.

After we were married, Matt and I came back to his childhood home. He was hurt to find that his special tree had been broken down by severe storms, and the people living in the house had moved its big branches into the field nearby.

Later on, his father pointed out some other smaller mimosa trees growing in the field, trees that had apparently been "born" from the one the little boy had planted. Now I was living in my husband's childhood home, and I could see that there were many of these trees growing in the area where the dying mimosa tree had been laid.

How like Matt's life, I thought.

He was nurtured and cared for; he was lovingly influenced by people who cared enough to show him that Jesus is the Way, the Truth, and the Life. He grew into someone so full of life and love that he brought beauty to the lives of those who knew him. His heart's desire was to live, in all of its abundance, a life pleasing to God.

Matt was only twenty-two years old when he was "broken down by severe storms"—his body succumbed to cancer. Yet even in his earthly death, just as in his life, fruit is still being born. And I am confident that the Lord will continue to use for His glory the testimony of Matt's life. In a unique way, his little mimosa tree still lives—through all the younger trees that grew out of it.

Wondering and wide-eyed, I began to see more of the creativity and artistry of my Elohim. He was Creator. He was always reproducing His life in willing hearts. His life was evident in His creation. The more I got to know Him, the more He filled me with His life. And I wanted to share the life welling up within me. I wanted to share His love with those who didn't know.

God was continuing the good work He had begun in me, and despite the moments of pain and hurting, it was exciting to know God was faithfully recreating the likeness of His Son in me. It was also thrilling to see the Holy Spirit's work in the lives of others, especially in my close friends. To hear how God used Matt's ordeal to strengthen their hearts brought me joy and showed me more of God's power.

September 19

I went to hear a friend sing with the group Living Word a few weeks ago. He mentioned Matt. But more importantly, he spoke with Your power and love. His life is changed. He is not the same; he is the same, yet different. His life is a touching testimony of what You can do with one yielded to You. He said he believes You and Matt talked about the group when Matt went Home. He never told anyone, except me and Matt, of his desire to sing in such a group. The day after Matt died, he got a call out of the blue from a man wanting to know if he was interested in singing in Living Word for the summer. Several obstacles stood in the way, and he was not sure what to do. He had paid for summer school and didn't know if he could get any of the money back. He had a summer job he couldn't afford to give up. He had signed a lease on his apartment he couldn't get out of. But You wanted him to sing. And You found a way. By Monday someone had called to sublet the apartment. He was able to get three months leave from his job. He got back every penny he had paid in tuition. You continue to amaze me.

God *was* amazing me. And I realized He was not doing anything out of the ordinary—He was just being God! How often had I hindered Him by not letting Him be Himself in my life? How many times had I denied His Lordship and thwarted

His power through me? The times, I am sure, are too numerous to count. But God is faithful to continue the good work He began in us and carry it on to completion, until the day of Christ. He will not stop working in my life and through my life until He is finished—what an awesome truth! He was still creating in me, and I can clearly remember the night something new surged in my heart—like the beauty of spring blossoming through the last winter snow....

September 20

Tonight I felt like I could be "me" again.
The air is cool; the night is clear; and God loves me. I am secure in Him. Matt is secure in Him. I am free to be who I am ...the "me" that God made me!

Matt had completed his journey faithfully. My journey still had mountains and hills and valleys and crossroads left to be explored. I had the assurance God was with me, and as I yielded to His control, I would become who He had in mind for me to be. It would have to be His work in my life—nothing of my own doing—that would allow me to live joyfully, abundantly, fruitfully.

After the fall semester began at Clemson, a friend of mine asked me to tell my story to a group of college girls. While thinking about what I would say to this Baptist Student Union group, several points became clearly outlined in my mind. I jotted them down....

Some things I am learning
About God...
1) He is sovereign, in control—always.
2) He is faithful.
3) He loves me—unconditionally.

About me...
1) I am weak; I am nothing without Christ.
2) I am not my own.
*3) I must trust God and obey Him—His love and
    wisdom merit my trust in Him.*

About others...
1) Others are watching
—to see how I handle it: attitude.
—to see how I am going to make it: actions..
—to see what is behind my attitudes and actions.
*2) Others may be going through something
    similar; they may need advice or friendship.*
3) Others are there to help me—let them.

About what to do...
1) Look to Jesus; spend time alone with Him.
*2) Seek what God is teaching through my trial—
    through prayer, through the Word, through
    counsel of wiser Christians.*
3) Rejoice and be thankful; there is victory!

My heart was beginning to rejoice again. At times I sensed not only the victory that is mine in Christ Jesus, but Matt's victory, too. He was somehow with me. I remember the night of his high school reunion; Matt's longtime friend Mark asked me to go with him. Matt had been student council president, and I knew he was known and loved by the students and faculty of Belton-Honea Path High School. What would the reaction of his high school friends be to his death? Would they be able to understand the true victory of knowing Jesus?

September 28

Matt's five-year high school reunion was a few weeks ago. I went with Mark. It was so strange to meet the people Matt had often talked about, the people who had known him longer than I had, the people who were with him throughout so much of his life.

I talked with several of them. I watched. I listened. I looked at pictures. Somehow, I could relive some of Matt's high school years with him. We were there together going through the memories. And inside I cried. How different it would have been if he were still here.

Mark read the letter to the senior class of '82; Judy had found it in one of Matt's school notebooks. He hadn't done anything with it before he graduated, but it contained a special message that needed to be said to some people who were dear to him. How he loved and cherished his high school years! We all cried when Mark read the words Matt had written with so much of himself.

Dear Seniors,

As this year draws to a close I feel that I must empty out my heart to you about my feelings about you. I've grown so close to all of you; you feel like brothers and sisters to me. There will always be a place in my heart in which I will hold all of those special memories that you have given me. In our lives there comes a time when we must let go of those things that we love, and the time has arrived that I must let you go. I feel like a part of me will be leaving with you and will struggle to remain a part of your life. As you go about your busy lives you will probably forget me, but I will continue to remember you and my prayers will go with you that you may receive life in its abundance, for it's what you deserve.

May God richly bless your lives, for you have blessed mine greatly with your mere presence.

Love, Matt

The rest of the night was anticlimactic...the music blared, people smoked and drank, everyone mingled. I didn't feel like I belonged there. Yes, it would have been so different if Matt were still here....

Things would have been different if Matt were still there. But what good would dreaming and wishing for him to be back do? Would I not drown myself deeper in sorrow and self-pity by dwelling on his death and absence? Instead, I wanted to be drawn closer to Jesus. He was the only One who could make something of my broken and hurting life. It was through Him and Him alone that I could find victory over Matt's death and move on in my life.

As God was healing my heart and opening my eyes, I began to notice more of His beauty all around me. Clear, blue skies; gentle, cool breezes; gorgeous sunrises and sunsets. I was able to see through the psalmist's eyes, "The heavens declare the glory of God; the skies proclaim the work of His hands" (Psalm 19:1). Everything was created to praise and glorify its Creator. His touch filled every day with joyful music and caused my heart to overflow with song. Praising Him brought new life to my spirit, and I wanted to know Him more.

"And this is eternal life, that they might know the One true God and His Son Jesus Christ" (John 17:3). So in this there is victory—eternal life!

Through a mutual friend I heard about Wanda's salvation. She had been living apart from God, and when a Christian counselor confronted her with her spiritual condition, she became defensive. Then the counselor mentioned Matt. Wanda and Matt had known each other all their lives, and they had graduated from high school together. She broke down and cried when the counselor asked her if she knew him. Matt had always been kind and caring, a good friend to her. He was an influential and godly example for her. Why had she strayed so far away from the God who loved her so much? The God who shone so beautifully through Matt Locke?

Wanda turned from her sin and committed her life to Jesus Christ. When I heard about her conversion, I wanted to meet her and talk with her. We finally caught up with each other—over the phone. It was no coincidence that I was finally able to reach her on that sunny October afternoon....

October 4

Earlier today I made a new friend over the telephone. We talked for about twenty minutes and made plans to get together tomorrow. She seemed so eager to know God and had a fresh thirst for righteousness. Now she is being tested.

I went to her house tonight. Death had been there. There were many tears and confused expressions. Thoughts of "why" and disbelief conveyed the unexpectedness of this tragic and unwanted event—her father had dropped dead of a heart attack only hours before.

Even though I taste and feel and experience the pain from Matt's death, I could not say anything. A hug, an "I love you," and an "I'll be here" were all I could manage. My body and expression were numb.

Life is short in this world. The brevity of life prompts me to commit every moment to You. You are still Lord. You are still in control. In this life we will always have tribulation and tears and heartache. We will be disappointed every day—You warned us of that. But You have promised us heaven. Oh, blessed and glorious Lord! You are heaven!

(later)

It was a year ago today...Matt and I were together with Lynne and Jim. We were laughing and having a great time. We ate cereal for breakfast. We went to a ball game and then a concert. A good memory.

And then...it was our first Sunday at Pope Drive. Matt was youth director, and I was so proud of him! I still am.

Tonight...I talked to Lynne and Jim. They remembered. And David and Michael Locke sang "Friends." David dedicated it to Matt. Russ gave his testimony. Ben was there, too. I love those boys.

I face the week ahead totally unprepared. But school is not so important now. Only Jesus and others matter. Where is the time to do all that needs to be done for You, Lord? I trust You have provided all the resources for me to accomplish what I need to— designed in Your will. Time included.

Yes, God provides everything we need to do His will. If any doubts arise about the possibility of living a life in the center of God's will, Jesus is always God's *yes.* I knew that "I can do all things through Christ who strengthens me"

(Philippians 4:13), but I often found myself trying to do too much. I so wanted to experience life to the fullest and invest myself in precious time with precious people. As Matt had done and—a greater example—as Jesus had done, I wanted to squeeze the most out of my limited time on this earth. Suddenly, I did not have much time for being quiet and still.

My body grew tired of the constant motion. I lived my life in three different cities—home in Honea Path, church in Anderson fifteen miles away, school in Clemson forty miles away. When could I rest? The physical exhaustion was reflective of the spiritual and emotional exhaustion. Inside there was a struggle—wanting to remain strong and steadfast in the Lord, yet at the same time wanting to be weak and coddled. I wanted to shout to the world of God's strength and power and love, and yet at the same time I wanted to cry out that I was hurting deeply.

It seemed that my humanity dictated my actions entirely too often. Sometimes I felt moody, apathetic, and withdrawn, and it was a real struggle even to try to let my light shine before men, that they may see my good deeds and praise my Father in heaven (Matthew 5:16). But through the blindness and confusion of my personal feelings, I realized the power of living by faith. "The righteous shall live by faith," not feelings. As an eagle soars above the storm, my spirit rose to believe in the Lord's Word. He gave me faith to know He would continue the good work He began in me, faith to trust Him to supply every need, faith to stand on His Word as I carried out my part of His plan. It is precious to learn to trust Jesus through all the feelings. When He is Lord of our lives, He is Lord of our feelings, too.

Admitting those feelings to Him—pouring out my heart to Him—was a release. He freed me from trying to be or do something I was not or could not do apart from Him. Though my omniscient God knew all about me, I found such peace in talking things out with Him—even when I thought I didn't want any comfort.

October 14

Oh, God, let me cry. I don't want any comfort right now. I just want to cry out to You, tears streaming down my face, holding my heart, feeling the pain. And then when I've finished crying and the last little teardrops have blurred my eyes, I want You to hold me like a small child and rock me and tell me everything is going to be all right.

(later)
Silence. The ticking of the clock is the only sound. With each tick my mind is brought back to another time, another place. A time when you and I could experience each other. A place where you and I could be together. Your smiling face. Your loving ways. Your "preciousness"—memories. Memories of when we first met, and you did a silly handshake. Memories of getting to know you and growing in love with you before I realized I was doing it. Memories of becoming engaged and marrying and our first night together. What a joyful time we had! And then....

The pain jars my body, my soul, as I remember these are now only memories. Only memories? They are yet more. They are a part of my life, a part of me...as you will always be.

It was a year ago today that I received that dreaded phone call. "Something is wrong." Were you meant to suffer so? A death that was stretched out over eight months, and yet in the midst of that dying there was so much life wanting to be lived.

It still doesn't seem real that we will never be together in the same way again. I cannot love you the way I desire to. You are here in many ways, and yet you are not.

God. Almighty God. I am in Your care. You are my Husband now. My Provider, my Love, my Friend. So much more than You were to me before. For I have experienced a complete relationship with another human being, a reflection of my union with You. Thank You for Your unconditional love.

Though I was truly satisfied with the fulfilling love of Christ, I longingly remembered the intimacy of our human relationship. Longing to be held, to nestle my head on Matt's chest, to cry in his arms—knowing him so well, knowing he knew me. Every day we spent together, we were continually learning about knowing each other and loving each other. All of that died with him. The things I could learn of him now would only be things of the past. And he was no longer there for me to give my love. Although my heart ached for what I could no longer experience, my focus was turning to God. I knew I needed to be continually learning to know Him and love Him.

God had sent some beautiful friends into my life; He surrounded me with people who loved Him. Martha had been more "a friend of a friend" through my college years. But God used our acquaintance as the starting point of a beautiful friendship that grew rich and deep. Long walks, captivating conversation, laughter. Martha was another bright light in the path that was often darkened by memories of Matt's suffering and death. She saw God's work in my life and encouraged me to walk ever closer with Him.

Lively and energetic yet also quietly pensive, Martha was known to have dreams that relayed some spiritual significance. One day as we walked along a narrow, winding road beside the lake, she related to me a strange dream she had the night before. At one point in the dream, her eyes scanned a dry, dusty desert. She saw it as if she were somehow standing outside the view. In the middle of this barren landscape was a little flower garden with bright, radiant blooms. Suddenly, a radio newscaster's voice broke through the quiet with shocking words.

"Lisa Locke died today...."

Martha was startled at the announcement, but as I listened to what she heard in her dream following the news of my death, I was humbled and thankful.

"...her life made people thirsty for God."

How I wanted to be the true salt of the earth! To make people thirsty for more of God, to be a reflection of His light in the darkness—only Jesus Christ could do that in me.

I remembered His warning in Matthew 5:13: "You are the salt of the earth. But if the salt loses its saltiness, how can it be made salty again? It is no longer good for anything, except to be thrown out and trampled by men."

It could have been so easy to withdraw from the world, to blame God for taking away the most precious part of my life, to waste my time lamenting what could have been. So many people do when they lose a loved one or go through trials and tribulations. But I realized that God was using the trials and tribulations to make me more of who He wanted me to be. He was using my life—and Matt's death—to bring glory to Him. He was using us to make people thirsty for Him. And that was what we both had always wanted.

As autumn leaves were slowly piling up on the brown, drying grass, my thoughts turned back to the scenes of a year ago. Some of my mind's images were so vivid that I could actually hear, sense, feel, see all that went on in those memories of mixed emotions. Anderson Hospital, the plane flight to D.C., the ambulance ride to NIH, people—loving, caring, kind people. I was drawn back to the place where it all happened. I wanted to go to Bethesda.

Bethesda. The name means "House of Mercy." Matt and I had surely been shown mercy there—God's love and the love of precious friends were real to us through the pain, darkness, joy, and light. I wanted to see my friends. I wanted to go back to the place where so many changes had occurred in my life. What would it be like to return to Bethesda? I had to find out.

With a few cancelled classes and some cuts to spare, it was easy for me to take off the first weekend in November. I purchased my plane ticket with a quiet excitement, anticipating good things about the trip—time with my friends, the beautiful autumn landscapes, showing the people there I was okay. Could God show them His love and power through my life? I prayed that He would. No good thing could come from my life by my own power. If they were to see even a mere glimpse of strength, joy, and comfort in me, I knew that it would be God's handiwork.

November 5

I'm on a plane to D.C. via Charlotte. Going back. Back to a place that holds so many memories. Memories that are painful and joyful. Mixed emotions? Not really. I am excited to see my friends who shared a precious and beautiful time in my life. With them I do not have to explain. They were there. They know....

(later)
Blank. Why am I blank? Is it a numbness to the emotions surrounding this trip? Or a protective shield placed by my Protector? I am very tired. My body feels weak and unrested. My mind is tired, too. Tomorrow I will see what it's like. For now I am just happy to see my friends and to know that God loves me. Thank You, Lord. You are beautiful!

November 6

Loved and assured. I feel warm and cozy. My heart is full of You, Lord, and I thank You. There is no sadness. Only the joy of Jesus. It is easy to experience that fullness that comes from only You when I am here alone with You. Thank You for being my Lord, Lord of my life, Lord of my heart, Lord of my being...and thus, Lord of my feelings. My life is in Your hands. I died, too, and my life is hidden with Christ in God. Thank You for the warmth of Your love.

November 7

There have only been twinges. Little shocks of pain in my heart, something like the charge caused by dry air in the winter, like rubbing one's feet on carpet and touching someone. But those twinges have come from hearts touching each other—sharing feelings, talking out needs.

November 8

I feel good today. I went to the hospital. Driving there seemed routine. A shaky feeling hit me when I got on the elevator. As I walked through the lobby with slow, measured steps, I glanced around. Nothing much had changed in five months. Nervousness right in the pit of my stomach. I rode the second set of elevators up and the same elevator lady was there—she didn't recognize me. Shakiness as I approached the doors to the thirteenth floor corridor. I walked deliberately to the nurses station toward familiar voices, a familiar place. They were surprised, but happy to see me. A few of the same staff remaining. Short conversations with everyone.
Thank You, God, for Your strength. I love You.

November 9

What a day! Flew home...looking forward to sleep and rest in You, Lord. Cleanse my spirit with a refreshing wind and wash it in the Lamb's blood. Forgive me for putting busyness into my schedule. Thank You for Your love. Thank You for being Lord.

"I am the Way, the Truth and the Life," He said. And just because truth is not believed by some does not make it any less true. Standing on the truth of His love for me and the reality of His presence in my life, I knew I could trust Him to lead me. Even when I could not see where I was going—"I am the Way." Even when my mind and heart were confused and muddled—"I am the Truth." Even when memories and thoughts of death crept into my mind—"I am the Life." His Word stood when I could not.

November 11

I found our marriage certificate stuffed in with some bills and papers. That was okay. That was happy. But tucked in the envelope behind our marriage certificate was another slip of paper. I unfolded it—his death certificate. Death—what an ugly sounding word. Dead. He is dead. No. He's not dead. He's alive in Christ. Though death sometimes seems so ugly—it is the enemy—we who know You, Jesus, can welcome death as the door to Life. Eternal Life with You. Thank You for the victory. You are incredible!

The excitement of His life in me gave me hope for new dreams. My life was going on! God was moving me through this process of discovering Him. Again I was thinking of my family and home in Alabama. I was delighting myself in Him—was He putting the desires in my heart to move home? Seeking wise counsel from several mature Christians, I was confident God would show me.

November 13

I have talked to a few others about going back to Alabama. What is pulling me so strongly? They have all said, "Yes, you have to do what you have to do." Profound. But I don't want to be led back by my emotions, nor my intellect. Rather, I must be drawn back, led to the place I need to be by the Spirit! By the Spirit. He is my Comfort and my Guide.

November 16

Lord, I am intensely drawn to You. I see You everywhere—in so many ways, in so many things. Thank You for the realization today...I won't forget. I was listening to some beautiful music, and I was filled by Your love and presence. Looking up at the mirror, I noticed the picture of Matt; he was smiling at me. The thought that he gave up his life so I could know You better came clear to me. Although it was not really his choice, I know Matt would have chosen to die for me so that I could know You in a deeper, total-surrender way. My eyes filled with tears.

I pondered that thought throughout the day, and then I realized—Jesus did that for me, too. He died so I could know and love You in a deeper, total relationship. Thank You, Lord. And thank you, Matt.

With Senator Strom Thurmond in Washington, D.C.

As the cool freshness of fall eased into cold, clear days, I thought about my family, turkey and dressing, football games. I was going home for Thanksgiving, and I couldn't wait. Although winter was fast approaching, my life was experiencing the newness of springtime.

November 26

Home—at last. Thank You God for a safe trip.
I've been reading a devotional book by Oswald Chambers. He encourages and exhorts a focus on the Cross of Christ, God Incarnate, Jesus Christ—a baby, a

Perfect Life, crucified...for me. These thoughts have been brought to my mind a lot lately. You amaze me God. I cannot understand the incredible truth of Your love, Your redemption plan.

Lord, teach me more about You. I want to know. I want to grow. My deepest desire is to love You, Lord, with all of my heart, soul, and mind. Continue to break me of my own will. I give it all to You.

November 28

I'm trying to discern what Your next step for me is—and You continue to teach me new truths. The other day I was talking to a friend about Your direction for my life, and she mentioned going where You could use me most. That thought rolled around in my head for awhile, then You revealed a bit of truth to me: I am not here to seek where You can best use me. I am not here even to be used by You, although that is the result of the reason I am here. Where You can use me best is Your decision; Your work is ultimately Your responsibility.

No, I am here first and foremost to seek Your kingdom. I am to love You with all my heart, soul, and mind. I am to obey You. As I die to "self"—as I am emptied of myself and drawn to You—only then can You use me. The realization brought to mind something I heard a pastor say, "We shouldn't pray, 'God, use me.' Rather, we should pray, 'Lord, make me usable.'" I am Yours, Lord. Make of me what You will.

While I sought God's direction for my life, I noticed a tangle of feelings, a struggle between what had been and what no longer was there. Though I was secure in Christ, my feelings flip-flopped from pleasant happiness to tearful sadness as I remembered. Sometimes my heart would cry, but tears would not come. I felt lonely, but I usually didn't feel comfortable in sharing my heartache with anyone. Why did I always feel like I would bother people if I turned to them in pain? Maybe it was a holy nudge from God, to cause me to come to Him first. The Lord of my heart who knew me better than I knew myself was enabling me to drink from His river so that I might live by His Spirit.

December 23

I feel alone. But You are here. You touch me and remind me of the reality of Your presence. You bring joyful music to my mind and cleanse my heart of this emptiness, filling me with You. Jesus. Jesus. Jesus. I want to know You more. Teach me to live like You. For I cannot of myself. No—live through me. Teach me to die like You first. All that I am is Yours.

A commitment to Christ demands a total sacrifice, completely giving ourselves away to Him, as He gave Himself away for us. It awes me to think our Redeemer counted us worthy of His death. Not only in death did Christ "give His life," but He gave His life every day He walked on this earth.

As the celebration of His birth approached, I thought about Jesus' selfless life, lived in perfect obedience to the Father. He gave His life. And He continues to gives His life for us to know Him.

December 24

Christmas Eve without Matt, yet with a deeper sense of the meaning surrounding this holiday. I cried this morning. I missed my husband, but most of all I missed my friend today. Matt was my best friend, and I wanted to share today with him, in person. I'm thankful for You, Jesus, and that we have a thousand eternities to share together—forever with Matt, forever with You. Sometimes those thoughts are all I need to be lifted above the world's drudgery. "I will praise the Lord who counsels me. Even at night my heart instructs me. I have set the Lord always before me. Because He is at my right hand I will not be shaken."

December 25

Christmas Day 1987. Quiet and still and thinking about You. Psalm 18—"I love You, O Lord my strength. You are my rock, my fortress, my deliverer, my refuge."

I talked to the Lockes this morning...and cried. Remembering last Christmas, our first Christmas together...and our last. Here on earth, anyway. What a beautiful memory!

Thank You, Lord Jesus. Thank You that You became a baby so I might know Your love. You who created all the things, the Giver of every good and perfect gift, created Yourself in human form and gave me the greatest gift of all—Yourself.

I love You, Jesus. And I'm confident Matt is by Your side, praising You eternally. I'll be there one day, and we'll worship You together—forever! Merry Christmas!

I had already decided not to continue with graduate school in the spring semester. God had made it clear to me that I was to go home to Alabama. I decided on a creative way to let my family know about it. With brightly colored Christmas paper, I wrapped a computer disk and secretly laid it under the tree.

On Christmas morning, the small, neatly wrapped disk was the last present to be opened. We all went to the computer and opened the file. Under "Christmas 1987" I had typed this "gift."

> *You may have heard rumors, but I want to tell you*
> *a few of my New Year's predictions...*
> *Becky will have more clothes to wear.*
> *Joe will have someone else to pick on.*
> *Sandy will visit more often.*
> *Mom will have more help (or hindrance) around*
> *the house.*
> *Dad will have someone to talk Clemson football*
> *with.*
> *I believe, as God leads, these things will come*
> *true.*
> *Merry Christmas!*

It took them a few minutes to figure it out. I was moving back to Florence. I was moving back home.

I was enjoying the time with my family, but even more, I was enjoying my time with the Lord. Relieved that He had guided me to a decision about the future, my spirit felt free to contemplate all that had happened over the past year.

December 30

Therefore, since I am surrounded by such a great cloud of witnesses, I must throw off everything that hinders and the sin that so easily entangles, and I must run with perseverance the race that is marked out for me. I need to fix my eyes on You, Jesus, the Author and Perfecter of my faith, who, for the joy set before You, endured the cross, scorning its shame, and sat down at the right hand of the throne of Your Father God. I will consider You who endured such opposition from sinful men so that I will not grow weary and lose heart. There is such power in Your Word. Every word of Yours is flawless; You are a shield to those who seek refuge in You. In You and You alone I will find my refuge and my strength.

I am dealing with "letting go's," and Your Word is an encouragement to me. I will find my hope in You, trusting in no man, leaning not to earthly wisdom. This one thing I do, letting go of what is a part of the past that will hinder what lies ahead, and pressing on toward the mark of the upward call of God in Christ Jesus. In order to hold on to You, Lord, I first have to let go of those things I am holding on to now.

I can no longer grasp those things that were a part of my relationship with Matt—You are calling me on. You have given me treasures to carry with me always— memories, thoughts, eternal truths, precious things about him that will never be forgotten. But I am beginning to see that I can no longer cling to what was. My dreams, my hopes, my life are in Your hands. I will cling to You. I am bonded to You eternally through the blood You shed for me.

Thank You that You count me as Your child. As I seek You, I am confident that You will draw me to You and fill me with Your Love. I am an open and broken vessel, humbled in Your presence. I want to be near You always, one with You, knowing You as You desire for me to. Thank You, Lord Jesus, for choosing me. I love You!

Love, Lisa

December 31

The year 1987 is swiftly slipping away. How can I express the depth of emotions I have felt this year, and what this year has been for me? I will remember this as the year of my precious husband's entrance into our eternal home—heaven! A year of great sorrow and, at the same time, great joy. Learning, growing, drawing closer to You. Groping, struggling, stumbling. Through it all You have been faithful. Your words are true and strong, and You have made them real in my life. For that I am eternally grateful. I am bonded more strongly to You through all You have brought me through.

Everything You choose for me, I humbly accept, being confident that You will continue Your good work in me until that day of Christ. I love You, Lord, and I will look to You for my strength, my hope, my security. You are my Source for all that is true and honorable and pure and lovely and admirable. The things that are excellent and praiseworthy come from You. Thank You for drawing me close to You and holding me there. I am anticipating great things in 1988....

Some new friends from a local church's college ministry invited me to "ring in" the new year with them. I don't remember the actual moment 1987 came to a close, but I knew God held 1988, which meant 1988 held good things for me.

January 1

And so begins another year.... This year will be different. Matt will be a part of it only in thought—in memories, in pictures, in sharing about his beautiful life. But Lord, I know that I could not go on—I wouldn't want to—without Your love, Your hope, Your control in my life. A new year would be scary if my security was in other things. But You are my rock, my fortress, my shield. Thank You. My love for You fills my heart—and even that is from You. Welcome, 1988.

January 8

A little seed of truth has taken root in my heart, and the possibilities of its growth excite me. God's wisdom and love merit our trust! So simple, yet at times so hard to apply. He is the all-knowing, all-seeing, all-powerful, all-everything. He is Sovereign. His love for us is unconditional and immeasurable. He will not lead us astray. He knows the thoughts He thinks toward us— thoughts of peace and prosperity. He knows the very best for us. We can trust Him with our lives. No fear, no insecurity, no confusion are found here in His gentle and loving hands.

Oh, God, please allow the roots of this truth to grow deeper! I am still learning what faith in You is all about. I love You! I am so unworthy of Your love for me...But Love is who You are, and I could never do anything to keep You from loving me. That thought brings me peace and strength. Thank You, Lord.

I had planned to return to South Carolina after the holidays to prepare for my move back home. A heavy snow— heavy for northwest Alabama—postponed my trip by several days. Although I was anxious to get on with my plans, I knew the Lord would show me how to walk in His timing.

January 25

Sometimes I don't want to wait on You, God. I know Your timing is perfect; I know You know what is best. But I am filling up with life and energy, and I don't want to waste any of it! I am eager to go, to do, to see, to experience, to love—but I must "be" first. I must be totally committed to You. I must die daily to all these desires and remember that only in You is my satisfaction to be found. Only You can satisfy the longings in my heart for someone to love. And only when I am fully Yours can I truly give of myself to others. My deepest desire is to please You. But desires are nothing without a commitment lifestyle to back it up. Yet even these are from You. The desire, the willingness, the commitment, the life—mine—are all Yours. May the words of my mouth and the meditation of my heart be pleasing to You, O Lord. You are all in all.

The trip back to Honea Path was peaceful, and my last weeks as a resident of South Carolina were abundant with time alone for me and my God. I invested hours in praising Him with music and song. I read the Bible. I enjoyed being with friends. How sweet it was to not live by a schedule. Jehovah-Jireh had provided for all my physical and material needs, and now He was providing for much-needed time alone with Him. Sweet and beautiful moments with Him. His time for me to move on was coming ever closer, and I wanted to enjoy all I could about the place I was in before pressing on.

February 9

I've wanted to do this for a long time now, but today the time is right. Sitting on the dock at the pond— a beautiful day—with my pen and paper, my guitar, my thoughts—and my Lord. What a gentle, cool breeze is blowing. The ducks are chattering across the way. The birds are chirping. Leaves are rustling. And You are calling me. Calling me on to a new chapter.

How can I express what I feel? Trying to allow the excitement of what is and what is to come to overshadow the sadness of what was and what will never be again...letting go of feelings, people, things, places—and holding on to You—Your love, Your wisdom, Your grace. Matt will always be a precious part of me. How very beautiful it is to know that. My eyes are welling up with tears, and the lump in my throat is hard to swallow.

I trust You, Lord, through the tears and through the pain. I trust You, Lord, to make me whole again.

(later)

I find myself wanting to hold on to this moment. Wanting to capture and remember these feelings. What are they? Sadness. Excitement. Mourning. Anticipation. Trust. Hope. Faith. Peace. And in the midst of it all is Your Love. Holding me, guarding me, guiding me. Thank you, Lord Jesus. Thank You for one of the most adventurous, deeply emotional, and even exciting chapters of my life. Where do we go from here? I don't know, but I want You to lead the way.

February 11

I'm here at the old house. One of my earthly homes. Sitting in my "God's lap" chair. As I sit here, I'm thinking about the words to "Faith-Walkin' People." When I went to the pond Tuesday with my guitar in hand, I decided to drive down. I got the car started and that song came on the radio. From beginning to end, from the time I started the car until I

*pulled onto the dirt road near the pond, You were
speaking to me as the words echoed the feelings of my
heart.*

*"Say goodbye to the feelings
'cause the feelings go away.
Say goodbye to the people
'cause the people never stay.
Say goodbye to the future
if it blinds you to today.
Say goodbye to the reasoning
that's standing in the way.
Oh, we've got to break away.... "*

Thank You, Lord, for what You are teaching me.

Love, Lisa

Wanting to break away from all that would hold me back
from being wholly His, I was realizing again and again my
nothingness. He is my life blood. Too often I do not think of
the significance of His blood shed for me.

He died, poured out His blood, for me. Broken, bruised,
and beaten, He gave blood freely flowing—His blood—for me.
His love and sacrifice broke me and encouraged me to follow
Him steadfastly.

My days in Honea Path were winding down. My mother came
to help me pack my things; she ended up doing most of the
work. Sandy had invited me to attend a missions conference in
Texas with her the weekend I was supposed to move, and my

parents encouraged me to go with my sister. With the help of my brother, my parents would pack up my belongings and move them to Alabama.

I could see that God was protecting me from an emotionally difficult day. I did not have to be around to see the little warm house being emptied as our things—Matt's and mine—were loaded onto a big cold truck. Instead, I would spend a priceless weekend with my sister learning about God's work across the world. Before I left to meet Sandy, I did a lot of reminiscing.

February 29

Reliving moments, memories, some painful, some joyful past times. Packing up, finding cards and letters, a box of his things. Tears, laughter, jokes. Mom's here. Thank You, God. Your protection and security surround me. You are my refuge. Without You I could not live.

March 1

I finally cleared out "the corner." So many memories crowded into such small space.... Today, after rummaging through, throwing out, packing up, repacking, and taping, I was standing in my bedroom, thinking about the significance of this day—that moment—and the song "Friends" came on the radio....

God, You are my safe place, my security, my refuge. My hopes and dreams are in Your hands.

The retreat was a blessing, but I was anxious to get home. It felt good to be back in Florence. Yet I continued to ask myself, *what's next?* Something about being back at home made me realize, with a fresh and painful reality, I was single again. And I had to surrender any hopes or plans or dreams I had about remarriage. I knew it was foolish to even think about loving another man right now, especially since I was still so deeply in love with Matt. The pain of his death and the memories of our brief marriage were far too fresh. Even so, I missed the communion, the closeness, the companionship that he had brought to my life. I had to continually die to my own self-will, allowing Jesus to be my Companion, to fill the void in my life that Matt's death had left. It was up to Him to crucify all that was in me that was not pleasing to Him.

March 22

How I long for Matt's arms to hold me, to comfort me. I feel so alone. "Yet, You're always with me. You hold me by my right hand. You guide me with Your counsel, and afterward You will take me into glory. Whom have I in heaven but You? And being with You I desire nothing on earth" (Psalm 73:23-25). It is so good to be near You, God—so good. I love You! You alone are the strength of my heart—my refuge. Thank You.

I need You, Lord. This time of transition, this "moving on" in life is not always easy. I am slowed down by memories and thoughts of what I want. Cleanse me and purge me of all that hinders Your work in my life, no matter how painful it may be. I purpose to follow You wherever You may lead me. Lead on, faithful Lord....

Like one whose vision had been impaired finding restored sight, I saw the Easter season through new eyes. Pensively, I thought about His sacrifice. Joyfully, I rediscovered the miracle of His resurrection. What power God had displayed in overcoming death! This same power was in my life. How could I not rejoice?

April 3

It is Easter, and I must celebrate! I do not take for granted the life You have given me—for it is not my own. I have been bought with a price, a high price. Thank You, Lord Jesus, for giving everything You had for me. I love You, dear Lord. You are my Savior

Jesus, God-incarnate, made Himself nothing, took the very nature of a servant, became obedient to death—even death on a cross. And we must look at Him....

His eyes, full of love and compassion, seeing the good in me—in everyone—seeing the being that God is creating, seeing the pains and hurts and deepest needs—and doing something about them.

His mouth, speaking wisdom and love, saying only what the Father would have Him say—encouraging, teaching, loving words.

His ears, listening to the voices crying out for love and warmth, listening to the hearts of people, listening to the Father's voice in perfect obedience.

His hands and arms, reaching out in love and selflessness, touching the inner man with peace and hope, healing diseases, hugging children, drawing people to Himself.

His feet, going places some scorned Him for, going only where the Father led, walking on water, running toward those who needed Him, taking the straight and narrow path.

His heart, His life, surrendered in total obedience to the Father, poured out for you and me, overflowing with love, perfect love, unconditional love.

And yet, they mocked Him and spat on Him; they beat Him and whipped Him.

They pressed a crown of thorns on His head, the thorns digging into His skull causing precious blood to flow over His eyes, His mouth, His ears.

They hammered spikes into His hands and feet, pounding blows of hatred and anger, and His blood flowed.

They hung Him on a cross to die a cruel death because they did not understand.

"They"—no, "we"—did this to Him. He bore our sin on that ugly cross. He felt intense pain and suffering. He bled and died.

He saw all who misunderstood Him; He heard their abusive mocking; and yet, He continued to reach out in love, speaking words of one in complete submission to the Father, "I forgive you."

Your death conquered all of death—for the resurrection power of God brought You out of the grave so that we might have life and forgiveness, and so that we might know You intimately.

Jesus—perfect, holy, righteous. We need to see You. When we look at You—when we really see You— we can't remain the same.

Jesus said, "But I, when I am lifted up from the earth will draw all men to myself" (John 12:32). He continues to draw people to Himself as He is lifted up in ordinary lives. I saw how He used Matt's life in that way. And people, whether they remembered many of the things Matt did or not, remembered the person Matt was on earth. Loving, kind, unselfish.

The Clemson Student Government Association established an award in his memory. An award in the political science department was renamed in Matt's memory also. Both groups invited me to present those awards at their respective ceremonies in Clemson. Without hesitation, I packed up and headed for South Carolina. I stayed with the Lockes in Honea Path.

April 7

So many feelings stir my heart at my return to this place. Although it is good to see the Lockes and be surrounded by familiar things from a special time in my life, there is a "hole." I don't feel the loneliness or the emptiness—just the sense that there will always be a vacancy here never to be filled again, like the empty chair beside me at church or something. I don't know. It's hard to describe.

I was in Clemson the other day, at the Student Government banquet presenting the Matt Locke Award. How proud I am of him! I will present the other award on Saturday.

Thank You, God, for the many opportunities You've given me to experience real life. I love You!

The Author of Life was writing His story on my own life. He was showing me the wonder of Himself. Driving back to Alabama after the ceremonies, He filled my heart with a song of praise. Like a child grasping his father's hand, I could sense the strength and the security that came from holding on to Him. What else did He have in store? His mercies were new every morning.

"Because of the Lord's great love we are not consumed, for His compassions never fail. They are new every morning; great is your faithfulness" (Lamentations 3:22-23).

April 16

Though the sun shone brightly, the air was chilly as I walked down the path along the golf course. Some friends of mine were playing in the church golf tournament, and I hoped to catch up with them and watch a few holes of good golf. Shivering, I zipped up my jacket and stuck my hands in my pocket; it was colder than I realized. Good thing I had my jacket with me. I hadn't worn that jacket in weeks, and when I put my hands in the pockets, I felt something else stuffed in them. Carefully, I pulled out wadded up tissues and a neatly folded ten-dollar bill.

"Wow! Thanks, God," I said aloud.

I knew that He was doing more than just placing a little extra cash in my hands. He was teaching me, again, a valuable truth.

Three days before, I had lost a ten-dollar bill. While talking with some friends at their store, I had carelessly thrown it away when I emptied the crumbled up papers from my pocket. I was meeting one of those friends down on the course, and soon I caught up with him.

"Hey, Bob, let me tell you what God showed me this morning."

I related to him about finding the money. It was almost as if God said to me, "Whatever you have lost or whatever you think you've given up for My sake, I will replace with Myself and what I want to give you."

My thoughts focused on things or people I was forced to let go of—Matt, my country home, some of my independence as I moved back in with my family, my hopes and dreams....

"Oh, by the way," Bob interrupted my thoughts, "I found your ten-dollar bill in the garbage can at the store."

"Whatever you have lost or whatever you think you've given up for My sake, I will replace with Myself and what I want to give you—in abundance."

There is no need to cling to the things we think we want or think we have to have. There is no need to fear what we may have to give up for Him, what we may lose for His sake. We must trust Him with everything. Everything!

"Now to Him who is able to do immeasurably more than all we ask or imagine, according to His power that is at work within us, to Him be glory in the church and in Christ Jesus through out all generations, for ever and ever! Amen."

The truths He was revealing to me prompted me to write more diligently. And He spoke to me through my writing. Things I had not pondered before broke through my mind as I sat down to type. And I was learning some unusual lessons as I sat in front of the keyboard.

May 19

A strange thing happened today...I sat down to work on the book and began to look through my journal, flipping back through pages of my life, stopping on August 10, 1987. The entry began, "The day after." It did not register with me immediately, and I thought, "The day after what?" I turned back to August 9, 1987—my one-year wedding anniversary—our wedding date. How could I have not recognized it instantaneously? As I read the words I had written nearly ten months ago, my heart remembered...and cried.

Suddenly I was aware of the tape I had put in for background music. The words rang loud and clear, and tears came to my eyes as I listened. "With this ring I thee wed, and I give to you my life." It was a song Matt had sung in a friend's wedding. I had a cassette tape of him practicing the song, and I listened to it often after he died. Though the song wasn't sung at our own wedding, he had sung those words to me when we were looking for music for our own ceremony. It is a special song. A prayer of commitment, words of agapé love.

What are you telling me, God? Was it a reminder of the oneness Matt and I shared? Was it a reminder of the standard You have set for marriage, something to refresh my memory for what I want? Oh, God, please be clear to me. Remove the shades that block my vision from seeing only You. Draw me to You and allow me to drink from Your fountain of living water—only You can satisfy me. I trust You, Lord. I trust You with my rela-

tionships. I trust You to show me where my life is going ...one day at a time, moment by moment.

As the one-year anniversary of Matt's homegoing approached, I prayed God would show me how to spend the day. Clearly and spontaneously, His leading came to me. On May 26, I called the Baptist Campus Minister at the local university. They were leaving for their annual beach mission for the weekend, and I wondered if they had room for one more. He was delighted by the suggestion and said I could go. I was ready to leave with them at five the next morning. The trip was a real blessing.

May 27

"This is the day that the Lord has made, I will rejoice and be glad in it."

I have had the wonderful sense today of being lifted up in prayer and held in Your hands, Lord. Joy— my heart is full of Your joy. Thank You, Lord, for Your guidance. It is no mistake that You have me here in Panama City on this beach mission.

The day started early for me—a 4:00 A.M. wake-up. When I got to the Baptist Student Union, I went to the prayer room...and talked to You. Oh, God, how I thank You for those refreshing quiet moments!

A good trip down—and I am here. Here for whatever reasons You have called me.

I am thankful the Lockes are in Your care, Lord. May they know Your peace and joy, especially today.

This day—it means more to me than just another day. A few tears today, but not much sadness. Instead, I celebrate Jesus and the life Matt is living with Him—the life He has also given to me. I praise You, God, for Your beauty everywhere...the people, the sunset, the ocean waves. I marvel at Your creation, but more so at You. I love You, Lord!

May 28

Somehow the word "soft" describes this morning. I guess after the "hardness" of last night—the hard looks on the faces of those in darkness, the hard beat of the rapping and rock screaming from the creeping cars, the hard atmosphere, a weak covering of the underlying pain and hurt—it is a soft morning. The ocean waves gently lap the receded shore line. People stroll serenely up and down the beach. A light breeze cools the air warmed by the early sun. The skies are clear, and there is a freshness in the atmosphere. Thank You, Jesus, for the softness and for this time with You.

(later)
We walked on the beach tonight—moonlight shimmering, glimmering, shining like diamonds on the ocean, waves in rhythmic succession splashing against the warm sand. We passed by so many people engulfed in their own passions, engrossed in their desires, oblivious to the beauty around them. Couples making out, groups laughing and dancing, many young people stumbling around drunk. What's the point? Futility. What is their god? Vanity. No purpose or meaning.

Several thoughts went through my mind as I walked. I reflected on the day...witnessing on the beach,

Gigi praying with tears in her eyes to commit her life to You; Kay under conviction, but rejecting what we shared; Wendy's pretty smile and encouragement; Audrey, the elderly lady, who just wanted to talk; Martha in pain, going through a bitter divorce....

The crowds were out tonight, one big party, orgies everywhere. These people are so lost. They're walking around in deep darkness. They don't even know what makes them stumble. All around us—so much noise, so much emptiness, so much darkness, sin—separation from God.

Thank You, Lord Jesus, that I am not of this world. You have chosen me out of the world, so the world hates me. I love You, Lord. Thank You for Your protection and security.

The beach was wondrously refreshing, and I did not want to leave it. But I returned to Florence wondering what God had in store for the summer. He had brought me through so many seasons of change.

Reflecting on His Spirit at work in me, I thought about the turning of winter to spring to summer to fall. His hand touched each season with beauty and life. My seasons, my times were—and are forever—in His hands.

Fall

Flaming hues of yellow, orange, red decorate the hills. Interspersed with the soft jade tones of the evergreens, dotted with browns, sprinkled with reflected light—the horizon is brilliant color. And this is autumn.

A cool breeze gently drifts the leaves from their branches against a deep blue sky. A season filled with the brightness of color, and yet...a season of dying.

Only the creative Maker of the universe could have fashioned such a scene and filled it with spirit-meaning. Yes, I see it, Lord—there is beauty in death. It is only in dying that these leaves can realize this beauty, the lively colors of fall.

So it is with me, Lord. Only in dying can I realize the beauty of You in me. And in a different way, so it was with Matt. In his dying there is sorrow; there is pain; there is suffering. That is death. But there is also life, and beauty. He is safe now. He is with You. What could be more beautiful?

Winter

Sometime during the night the white flakes had fallen, and I woke up to a wintry snow-blanketed neighborhood. The scene seemed to hold some sort of excitement, and before the morning wore on, I bundled up and walked outside. The crisp, cold atmosphere was quiet and still. My boots made a gentle crunching sound just loud enough for me to hear as I trudged across the unblemished yard.

Was it just a year ago that Matt and I walked through the new-fallen snow at our temporary home in Maryland? He, though weakened by the cancer treatments, was strong enough to push me into the bushes, and we laughed.

The area had more snow than it was ready for, but we made the best of that cold, bitter winter. I remember slipping and sliding, buying waterproof boots, making snow cream.

It was fun, yet it was a wintertime in our lives, too. He was so sick and frail, but he always wanted to squeeze all the life he could out of every moment...until he breathed his last breath months later. Only God could comfort and strengthen. And He gave us the courage to smile and laugh and enjoy life—even in the wintertimes. He continues to do that for me.

Spring

Walking through the neighborhood this morning was refreshing. Bright flowers blooming, bare trees beginning to bud, blue skies, brilliant sunshine—it is spring! Spring, to me, brings forth feelings of new life, new birth, an invigorating excitement that makes me want to shout, "Thank you, God, for life."

I am beginning a new life now. Transitions and adjustments are here; I am in a different place with new friends and a freshness in my relationship to my God and King. Part of me died last spring. Though the earth was beautiful with a fullness and aesthetic quality I had not seen before, my precious husband's life was slipping away. His last breath came as spring faded into summer, and he passed into a new life, a better life where spring happens all the time. Jesus is there—that is the beauty of it.

Jesus is here, too. And He makes life beautiful for me. With Him I can have spring all year round.

Summer

Adventure. New experiences. Sunshine. Playing hard and working hard. Relaxation and leisure. Starting over...without Matt.

The summers of my life have been enriching, growing, learning times—something new every warm season. Yet he and I never spent a summer together. From the time we knew each other, summers found us separated, usually by hundreds of milest.

Reflecting on those summers, I realize the treasured memories of the growing times we had apart— together. Sharing in each other's lives through phone calls and letters, wanting to be together, knowing it was not yet time.

Both of us answered the call to summer missions— he went to the Grand Canyon in Arizona the summer I was in Arlington, Virginia. The following year I spent the summer on missions in Trinidad, Colorado; Matt was in summer school at Clemson. And the next summer we each spent with our families in preparation for our wedding.

How drastic were the changes in circumstances from the summer of '86 to the summer of '87. In '86, anticipating life together with the man I loved. Looking forward to realizing dreams together. Excitement. Energy. Exhilaration. In '87, grieving over his death. Looking back at the precious time we had together. Adjustment. Transition. Pain.

Now, here I am in the summer of '88. God has been faithful in holding me close to Him. He has shown Himself strong and loving. He has brought to my life comfort, peace, hope. Still, I look forward to realizing dreams. He has given me new dreams—with excitement, energy, exhilaration. Still, sometimes I look back at all He has brought me through, to special memories that will always be a part of who I am.

We all go through times of adjustment, transition, and pain. What determines our response to life's circumstances? We can choose to trust God, to take Him at His Word. We can believe He is continually working through all things for the good of His kingdom, for our good. We can have faith in knowing everything we are stepping through in this life is filtered through His loving hands. He is Sovereign. He is Lord. I have chosen to trust Him—not only in the summers of my life, but through every season.

"You have made known to me the path of life; You will fill me with joy in Your presence, with eternal pleasures at Your right hand" (Psalm 16:11).

EPILOGUE

Through the pages of my writing, through every line, I have relived a precious chapter of my life. Not only have I grown to know and love Matt Locke better, but I have also come to know and love my Lord Jesus in a more intimate way. All the while God is drawing me deeper into fellowship with Him, abiding in Him. He is calling me on, and I am learning to trust Jesus with all that I am, in all that I do.

He has given me many opportunities to share with churches, high school students, college groups, and children what He is teaching me.

Late one Friday night I was to share my testimony at a youth lock-in. The day had been exhausting after a trip to a nearby city and then a softball game. Trying to beat the ball to first base, I pulled some muscles in my leg. I was out for the rest of the game.

Around 11:00 P.M., I arrived at the church for the lock-in. Nearly a hundred young people were already there, laughing and playing games. Hobbling around the room, I felt the pain in my leg increase with every step. A few minutes before I was supposed to speak, I slipped into a quiet room away from the noise of the gym.

Kneeling down before my Father, I committed to Him what was already His and asked that my words be His words. I began to praise Him for His love, His goodness, His faithfulness. And as I did, a wonderful thing happened. I no longer noticed the pain in my leg. Not that my leg was healed, but the position I was kneeling in lessened the stress on my muscles, and *my focus was not on my pain.*

It was so simple. God was saying to me, "This is what I've been showing you for the past several months. When you take your focus off your circumstances, off your pains and disappointments and frustrations, and turn your focus to Me, everything else fades into the background. As you praise and worship Me, as you seek Me above all else, temporal things, earthly pain, and all other hindrances lose their place in your thoughts. You are able to take on more of My perspective and see the Big Picture I am painting."

Words to a familiar hymn flowed from my heart as I began to quietly sing, "Turn your eyes upon Jesus, look full in His wonderful face, and the things of earth will grow strangely dim in the light of His glory and grace."

As I went out to share my testimony with those eager young people, my heart was full of love for and thankfulness to my great God. Jesus—He is the light of the world. I read to them something which Matt had written several years before.

I see the dark clouds rolling in. Watching their movement bring them slowly closer; but I look at them with joy in my heart.

I just wish I could explain the joy which never departs, but it holds an unexplainable mystery to it. You see, I know what it's like to be able to shine when there is darkness all about you. It's not me that does the shining. It comes from within, from within a heart that has been grown by the following and surrendering to Another. Another that has endured the darkness when it was so dark that it could be felt, Another that felt pain which was brought on by those that He loved so. He was a man of great love, compassion, and understanding. The darkness tried to extinguish the light that burned in Him and it thought it had succeeded when it took His last breath. But a spark remained and this spark began to grow, in the very depth of darkness, and it burst forth with victory. It created a light so bright that it consumed the darkness. This is where my source lies. This light now burns within me. I dull its glow sometimes when I fail to fuel it each day, but it continues to glow, nonetheless, in spite of me, because it is rooted too deeply to be extinguished.

The Light continues to shine, in spite of all of us. But may we be ever mindful that the One who said, "I am the Light of the world," also said, "*You* are the light of the world." We are called to be reflections of that light—His light—no matter what the cost to us.

Matt Locke lived that light no matter what the cost, and he was happy to say with Paul, "For to me, to live is Christ, to die is gain...."

Dear Father,

Night has come and darkness has clothed the sky. I am alone in this big house, and the quietness of these moments draws me to You. You are with me always, and I praise You for Your peaceful presence. There is no greater love than Your love. Continually I find my refuge in Your name.

Memories of the past few years do not haunt me. Matt's suffering, death, burial. Rather, they cause me to reflect on Your goodness, Your provision in my times of great need. And I see more clearly how I need You all the time—not just in the times I call out to You in the weakness of my humanity, but in times of elation and excitement. I need You to cry with me and to celebrate with me. For what is this life but a journey through changes, obstacles, challenges, trials, surprises, struggles, joys? Each step draws me closer to You.

Lord, I think about all You have done for me. "This is what the Lord says, your Redeemer, the Holy One of Israel: 'I am the Lord your God, who teaches you what is best for you, who directs you in the way you should go.'" I am saddened by my compromise and settling for less than the best.

Yet You have shown me what is real and what is true. "For God was pleased to have all His fulness dwell in Him, and through Him to reconcile to Himself all things, whether things on earth or things in heaven, by making peace through His blood, shed on the cross" (Colossians 1:19-20). You took the initiative to reconcile me to Yourself. And I know You are continuing what You started in me.

Jesus, You are my Lord. Though I have stubbornly resisted at times, I have given You control of my life, and I know that my purpose here is to love You, to know You, and to obey the words You have commanded. I do not always understand what that means and why things happen the way they do, but I do know without a doubt that I can trust You. I must trust You. The fact that You are God demands it. The truth that I am Your child requires it. And even this trusting You is something I must learn more about day by day.

You are faithful, Lord. I believe what the prophet Isaiah said: "The Lord will guide you always; He will satisfy your needs in a sun-scorched land and will strengthen your frame. You will be like a well-watered garden, like a spring whose waters never fail."

I could have no better Guide, no greater Source of the wellsprings of life than Life Himself. You, Lord Jesus. You have given me this precious gift of life because You love me. As I reflect on your love, my mind is filled with thoughts of moments when I experienced Your gentle outpourings of Yourself.

May 27 this year was a day of reflection. While I shuffled through some boxes in the garage, I discovered some red ribbons, pressed flat from the long storage. I pulled them from the overstuffed box and noticed a card pinned to one strand of the wrinkled ribbon. As I stood in the middle of the garage surrounded by piles of boxes—his things, my things, our things—I slowly opened the worn envelope. A simple phrase bore a timely reminder. "Just because I love you—Matt."

He had given me so many gifts—cards, letters, a tender gaze, gentle words—just because he loved me. His greatest gift was himself. He gave himself to me, second only to giving himself to You. How I thank You, Father, for this most precious gift!

You reminded me again how his love for me is no less a part of my life because of what happened a few years ago. It will always remain because of what happened two thousand years ago. And again I must reflect....

"He humbled Himself and became obedient to death, even to death on a cross."

"...who for the joy set before Him endured the cross, scorning its shame...."

"Carrying His own cross, He went out to the Place of the Skull. Here they crucified Him...."

And You say to me, Lord Jesus, "Just because I love you."

How could I refuse so great a love as this who became sin for me that I might be made righteous in God's sight? How could I not submit and surrender to Your plans and ways?

Your ultimate design for me is to be conformed to Your likeness. Your tools in this process are not always painless. But as I surrender my will, as I worship You as my rightful Lord and Master, I find my reality.

Oh, faithful Lord, continue the work You have begun in me, no matter how painful. Like Matt, I too pray that You will do "whatever it takes." I am Yours.

Love, Lisa

William Mattison "Matt" Locke

About the Author...

Lisa K. Locke found herself a widow at the age of twenty-three. But she hasn't let that stop her from following Matt Locke's example of living life to its fullest. She has been involved in missions work both at home and overseas, and she has become a popular inspirational speaker to youth, college, and adult groups. She con-

tinues to fulfill Matt's dream of encouraging people to live each and every day in the only way that matters—for Jesus.

Currently, Lisa is completing a master's degree in education and communcations at Regent University which she hopes to use in working with young people. Lisa lives in Virginia Beach, Virginia.

Do you know someone who would enjoy this book?

VISION PRESS, INC., P.O. Box 1889, Cheyenne, Wyoming 82003

Please send me _____ copies of *Love, Lisa*. I am enclosing **$10.95 per book** (or **$9.95 each** for 3 or more copies), plus **$1.00** per book for postage and handling.

Name ____

Address ____

City _____________________ State ____________ Zip ________

Please send check or money order only (sorry, no cash or C.O.D.s).
For credit card orders, call toll-free (800)788-1889.
Please allow 4 to 6 weeks for delivery.

Price and availability subject to change without notice.   LL1-91